The Writer's Handbook

Jeff Griffith, M.A.T., M.L.A., Ph.D.
Professor of English
and
Coordinator of Medical Writing,
Community College of Baltimore

Donna Ignatavicius, R.N., M.S.
Instructor, University of Maryland
School of Nursing

The Complete Guide to Clinical Documentation, Professional Writing, and Research Papers

Resource Applications, Inc.
7250 Parkway, Suite 510
Hanover, Maryland 21076

(301) 796-9010

RESOURCE APPLICATIONS, Inc.

Resource Applications is a network of educators and clinicians committed to lifelong learning for health care professionals, and excellence in education.

Resource Applications offers:

A comprehensive program of continuing professional education.

An ongoing mechanism for updating clinical competence and professionalism.

A unique approach to education that "bridges the gap" between theory/research and clinical practice.

A unique network of talented clinical and management consultants from across the United States and Canada.

Publishing Director	Jay Katz, M.A.
Editorial Director	Jacqueline Katz, M.S., R.N.
Cover Design/Graphic Design	Janet Bowling
Production Assistant	Alicia Ludwick
Typesetting	The Graphics Group

ISBN 0-932491-37-5 Printed in the United States of America

In Loving Memory of my Dad, Barney Dennis
D.I.

To My Family: Maria, Leza, and Lynne
J.G.

Preface

The Writer's Handbook presents instruction in how to perform the major writing tasks required in health care settings. Our intent is to provide one source book which treats the most frequent, most common writing requirements.

Our approach has been to analyze the kinds of writing tasks most often required and to present step by step direction in how to proceed with them. We believe that one learns most readily when the material to be mastered comes in small, manageable steps; therefore, each chapter subdivides the writing process into small pieces, presents an overview, and then explains the process step by step. Each chapter includes samples of the desired product.

Our intended audience includes nurses, therapists, dietitians, physician's assistants, social workers, in short, anyone who works directly with clients in a health agency. Naturally, some elements of this book are more useful for some members of this broad audience than are others. Nonetheless, we've attempted to provide a range of examples and samples which, though they can't all be applicable to every variety of health care professional, will touch many. The examples clarify selected points.

We've intentionally avoided advocating one side or the other in certain cases where professional controversy exists. We express our view; you choose the approach you think works best for you or your agency.

The Writer's Handbook consists of three parts. Unit I, **Clinical Documentation,** addresses the kinds of writing tasks which are related to direct care. Chapter 1 presents skills for writing progress notes; Chapter 2 explains methods for writing assessments; Chapter 3 provides a systematic model for care plan development; Chapter 4 discusses a simplified step by step model for procedure development.

Unit II, **Writing in the Professional Setting,** focuses on writing tasks useful in various kinds of professional activities. Chapter 5 presents techniques for preparing an effective vita, resumé, and letter of introduction. Chapter 6 discusses methods of preparing and submitting work for publication. Chapter 7 simplifies memo and letter writing, explaining techniques for preparing effective communications.

Unit III, **Writing in the Academic Setting,** is a handbook on secondary research and research writing. Chapter 8 presents step by step instruction in topic selection and focusing, source selection, and note-taking, and also explains how to prepare precis. Chapter 9 continues with instruction on planning, organizing, documenting, and actually writing the research paper. This chapter explains how to use reference notes and how to prepare a bibliography.

The chapters progress in small steps, building incrementally and progressively on each concept. Generally, the chapters are themselves ordered so as to build upon each other. Exercises in, and at the end of, each chapter reinforce the skills and concepts discussed.

We have approached our writing task with the assumption that our audience is reasonably well informed in clinical content but less well informed about the process skills involved in medical-technical writing. We have attempted to assume nothing and to present the writing skills in each chapter beginning with the most basic. We hope you will find our efforts useful.

Jeff Griffith
Donna Ignatavicius

Table of Contents

PAGE

PAGE

Unit I Clinical Documentation

Introduction

Documenting the care you give your clients is as important as the actual care itself.

Why is documentation so important? In the event of a law suit, you must be able to prove that the care you gave met at least minimal standards. Unless a written record of that care exists, you cannot offer such proof. The assessment, care plan, and progress notes are the key elements of a comprehensive documentation package. Were you to be involved in a malpractice suit, the court's attitude would be, "If it's not in writing, it didn't happen." Even an eyewitness account that you'd performed a certain intervention would be unlikely to convince a jury.

Documentation is critical for continuity of care. A written record of the client's condition and of care given forms the barometer by which other health care professionals can monitor progress or deterioration in the client's status and evaluate the effectiveness of care delivered. Access to the data provided by each member of the health care team assists the other members to carry out individualized care. Displaying the assessment data, care plan, and progress notes of each member—nurse, therapist, dietitian, social worker—in the same package, forms a total picture of the client and the care he or she receives.

The four chapters which follow discuss aspects of writing about providing direct care. In Chapter 1, "Writing Progress Notes," you learn how to record the significant elements of the client's condition and your interventions. Chapter 2, "Writing Assessments," describes the various issues you must address in writing your assessment of the client's condition. Chapter 3, "Preparing the Comprehensive Client Care Plan," lists step by step the procedure for developing the care plan, from problem identification through monitoring the client's progress. Each of these chapters focuses on a piece of the documentation process. To some of you, this sequence, progress notes first, will seem wrongheaded. We've ordered the chapters this way because the writing skills implicit in progress notes are basic to the writing tasks involved in assessing and planning.

While the first three chapters focus directly on documentation, Chapter 4, "Writing Procedures," is more closely related to standards of care. Procedure writing produces two results, at least. First, the procedure prescribes step by step how to carry out a given task, direct care, administrative, or otherwise. Second, the procedure offers a concrete benchmark against which to compare the performance of the health care given. If documentation reveals that care conforms to standard procedure, then the burden of verifying effective care delivery is met.

Each of the following four chapters presents formats which you will typically find in various health care agencies. Since "paperwork" is such an important part of your professional responsibility, these samples should help prepare you for the actual types you'll use each day. Each chapter also presents samples of finished products for your review and offers exercises to help reinforce your learning.

Chapter 1
Writing Progress Notes

Objectives

After reading this chapter and completing the exercises, you should be able to document your interactions with your patients.

Specifically in this chapter, you learn to:

- Identify and apply the elements of narrative note and SOAP note processes.
- Identify and apply guidelines for effective documentation.
- Describe characteristics of ineffective documentation.
- Revise and correct ineffective documentation.
- Describe applications of various flowsheets and charts.

Progress notes are a component of the overall documentation of client care and a tool to provide communication, record keeping, and quality assurance. Progress notes provide an ongoing, timely record of a client's condition and of interventions by members of the health care team. These notes document assessment, planning, implementation, and evaluation. Additionally, the notes record the activities of therapists, social workers, dietitians, and other health care personnel.

Traditionally, source oriented notes, such as physician's progress notes, nurse's notes, therapist's notes, and so on, have been located separately within the client's chart. Now, however, the trend is toward comprehensive progress notes which include records from the entire health team. The policy of each health care agency determines who writes progress notes and where. For example, in some cases, nursing assistants independently document interactions with clients. In other instances, nursing assistants must obtain an authorized cosigner such as an R.N.

Policies and procedures vary. Hospitals and extended care, chronic care, home health care, and outpatient care agencies have certain unique requirements. The approach here is designed to be adapted to any environment in which documentation is needed.

How important are progress notes? The only record of the client's condition, and also a legal document, the progress notes are as important as any aspect of client care. They must be absolutely clear and perfectly accurate. Legally, an action or observation which is not noted in the record did not happen.

How To Write Progress Notes

The first question in all communication is "What does my audience need to know?" The next question is "What's the best way to get my message across?" Readers of progress notes need to know everything—about the client and about the actions of the members of the health care team—which enables them to work effectively with the client. Give your audience the essential facts but eliminate irrelevant information. Use the following guidelines:

1. Observe carefully; report observations in specific concrete language that appeals directly to the senses.
2. Record your observations and actions immediately.
3. Select detail carefully; develop each point fully.
4. Organize logically.
5. Write objectively.
6. Present notes in an accessible format.
7. Proofread.

Observe and report. Effective progress notes rely heavily on language that appeals directly to the senses, including quotes. Report what you see, hear, feel, and smell in terms as close as possible to the actual experience. Choose the most specific, most concrete terms available. Use standard professional terms only; use approved abbreviations only. Always choose, however, the simplest term that says what you mean.

Example:
An occupational therapist sees misaligned fingers.
The therapist records:

8-12-8-; 12 P.	Swan neck deformities, all digits of right hand.
	Jane Doerr, O.T.

Note the use of the analogy "swan neck" to enable the reader to visualize the deformity. In addition, to say that such a condition is "present" or "noted" is redundant—simply report your observation.

Example:
A nursing assistant hears a client say that the room is too hot. He takes the patient's temperature, checks the room thermostat, and records:

12-20-8-; 12 P.	States "This room is too hot." Room temperature 68°, client temperature 102°.
	John Buck, N.A.

Note that the nursing assistant reports both observations and results of actions taken. The direct quote of the client provides a clear context for the actions taken. The subject of states, "client," is clear and thus unnecessary to write. Do so only when clarity would otherwise suffer.

Example:
A physical therapist feels resistance to range of motion exercises during which the client is in pain. The therapist records:

2-5-8-; 11:30 A.	Achieved 80° forward flexion of right shoulder. Gritted teeth and frowned during exercises.
	John Smith, P.T.

Note that the therapist reports not that the client is "in pain" but rather reports visible evidence of pain.

Example:

Noting a client's swelling, her nurse records:

9-23-8-; 2 P. Spongy, smooth, quarter size, fixed lump on ulnar aspect right arm, 2 inches below elbow. Raised 1/4 inch.

Jane Seymour, R.N.

Here the nurse selects particularly concrete terms to describe the texture of the lump and records its size and location specifically.

Example:

9-16-8-; 4 P. Voided 100 cc. dark yellow, cloudy, foul smelling urine.

Ann Boley, R.N.

"Foul smelling" is probably as close as one can come to certain odors, since smells are extremely difficult to discriminate. If what you note smells like something else, use an analogy. Here the visual language, "dark yellow, cloudy," helps reinforce the odor.

Sensory based language is extremely effective in communicating clearly, as is analogy. The examples here illustrate concrete, specific language related to all but the sense of taste. The observer is unlikely to be able to use taste as a tool; however, client reports may be important. "Tastes like metal," for example, is a comment which could suggest a medication side effect and should be documented.

Table 1-1 lists some common terms to use and avoid when describing skin, wounds, lumps, and drainage.

Table 1-1

Sensory Descriptors

Skin
Visual and Tactile

Use:

white	smooth	sweaty
ashen	hard	oily
pallid	taut	greasy
opaque	drawn	scaly
silvery	tight	waxy
grey	dry	yellow
smoky	rough	chalky
cyanotic	flaky	milky
blue	clammy	pasty
orange	crusty	soft
sallow	diaphoretic	hot
jaundiced	leathery	warm
calloused	raised	cold
spongy	moist	

Avoid:

pale	normal
fair	livid
flushed	discolored
sunburnt	

Wounds
Visual and Tactile

Use:

color, texture, terms from list above.
size (in inches long)
size of a ____________
shape of a

pear	kidney
moon	boat
crescent	

round	jagged
even	open
closed	sutured
stapled	

filled with (gravel, dirt)
draining/not draining

Avoid:

healed	big	small
infected	medium	little
	tiny	large

Drainage
Visual, Tactile, and Olfactory

Use:

colors listed under skin
Sero-Sanguinous
Sanguinous
cottage cheese-like

foul smelling	gelatinous
alcohol-like	pungent
garlic-like	musty
bleeding	doughy
clear (serous)	tenacious

frothy	sour	gummy
bloody	sweet	musky
watery	oily	slippery
cloudy	fetid	rancid
purulent	pasty	greasy
viscous	fishy	fecal-like

Avoid:

thick	thin	rank
stench	smelly	shiny
funky	putrid	stinky
nauseating	offensive	reek

Lumps
Visual and Tactile

Use:

terms listed under skin
size of ____________

fixed	movable

Avoid:

big	large
small	medium
little	tiny

APPLICATION:
In the space provided, use specific sense oriented language to:

1. Describe a scar or wound on a selected client.

   ____

   ____

2. Describe the condition of a selected client's skin.

   ____

   ____

3. Describe an odor related to a selected client's condition.

   ____

   ____

Remember, select terms which appeal to the senses.

Record immediately. "I don't have time" is the plaint of many professionals who record their notes at shift's end or at some other time well after the fact. These same individuals, however, obviously have time to perform the other aspects of client care. Documenting care is as important legally as giving the care. If it's not in the chart, it didn't happen, so if anything is omitted from the progress notes, the care provider may later be unable to prove having met standards of care.

Timely documentation decreases the likelihood that important items will be missing, inaccurate, or garbled. Can you remember exactly what you were doing eight hours ago? Obviously, one's ability to recall detail diminishes over time, especially in stressful environments. Omissions are a major factor leading to lawsuits.

Make the time to document as you deliver care. If necessary, carry a reporter's notebook—a spiral flip pad—or a set of note cards and jot down key words. Later, you will be able to reconstruct your experiences more effectively and these informal notes may protect you legally. Never document before the fact, of course.

How frequently you chart routine observations depends on facts miscellaneous and various, such as the client's situation, institutional policy, types of care given, and requirements of regulatory bodies. In any case, record at once, but remember that some routine data appear elsewhere in the permanent record, on flowcharts, graphs, and check lists, and need not appear separately in the progress notes.

While progress notes report ongoing observations in sequence, occasionally summary reports are necessary to highlight the most important aspects of the client's course of treatment. The summary note provides the reader a capsule picture. Admission, transfer, referral, and discharge notes are common summaries. Admission notes frequently substitute for assessment forms in capturing the client's status on admission. Transfer notes describe the client's status at the point of transfer to another unit or agency. Referral notes provide other departments with information useful specifically to them. Discharge notes describe the client's status on completion of care in a particular agency.

Here is a sample discharge note for a patient who has been treated for hypertension:

Sample Discharge Note:

5-31-8-; 4:20 P.	B/P 132/84; T.98; P.88; R.16. Reviewed 2 Gm Sodium diet meal sheet and Na^+ restrictions. Reviewed Med list (Aldomet and Lasix) actions and side effects. Reinforced need for purchase of B/P cuff for daily B/P monitoring by wife. Client reports, "I understand my medications and diet. The dietitian talked to me this morning." Scheduled follow up meeting c̄ Dr. Jones in 2 wks; follow up consult c̄ J. Johnson, dietitian, in 4 wks. John Roberts, R.N.

Select and develop detail. Remember to ask, "What does my audience need to know?" Include everything you believe is important; when in doubt, include questionable detail. What's important? Signs; symptoms; behaviors; comments; interventions, including teaching;

response to interventions; physical status; emotional and mental status; spiritual needs; social status. Document whatever you regard to be significant. Be especially alert for changes.

Sometimes what is absent is as important as what is present. Report lack of postoperative bleeding, for example, and record the absence of drainage, dyspnea, dizziness, or any other expected problem which does not occur.

Example:

Document a problem free postoperative recovery, like this:

3-18-8-; 1:45 P. B/P 120/80; T 98; P 78; R 13. Midline abdominal dressing dry and intact. Bowel sounds diminished all quadrants. Abdomen soft. Bilateral basilar rales posteriorly. Coughing intermittently. Drinking 200 cc clear liquids $\bar{q}$ 2 h. Reports no nausea or vomiting. Foley catheter draining clear yellow urine @ 80 cc $\bar{q}$ h.

Donna Nash, L.P.N.

Many agencies remind professionals of what's critical by providing selection guides. The frequently used SOAP note structure, discussed later in this chapter, functions in such a way. Some agencies offer staff members pocket aids listing key elements; others post such lists for reference.

Entries such as "quiet night," "slept well," "resting quietly," or "tolerated procedure well" are worthless. Since they offer nothing significant, eliminate them. Eliminate redundancy as well. Classic redundancies include "cool to touch" and "pink in color." How could we tell if the patient's skin is cool without touching it? Pink is a color. Such wordiness wastes time for both the writer and the reader. Concentrate on presenting sufficient data in the fewest possible words but don't labor over conciseness. Skill at condensing information comes as a result of experience and discipline.

Avoid "appears," "seems," and their variants, since these terms warn your reader that you're unsure of your observations. "Appears to be sleeping" is useless information since sleep is not observable. "Seems confused" is similarly worthless. Confusion is an internal condition. Replace phrases like these with descriptions of observable behavior: "Supine, eyes closed, respirations regular" describes sleep; "Does not follow directions" or "Climbs over bedrails" may indicate confusion. The point is that describing behaviors is effective; labelling mental states is not.

Many widely used generalizations are similarly misleading: "cooperative," "depressed," "demanding," "friendly," "hostile," and similar labels communicate little but the writer's attitude. Write what you observe that leads to your conclusions about the client and avoid judgments. For example, "assists with dressing change" may be cooperation. "Crying," "avoids eye contact," "stares out window" may support depression.

Using sense based language to report observable behaviors is the critical element in presenting detail effectively. Concise, concrete language reinforces the effect.

When describing behaviors, avoid these terms as well as those mentioned above:

drunk	frustrated	hostile	active
sober	nervous	combative	fearful
alert	bad	confused	disturbed
unhappy	good	disoriented	defensive
distant	indifferent	happy	disruptive
aloof	normal	uncooperative	jovial
tired	abnormal	comfortable	sad
exhausted	calm	uncomfortable	appropriate
sleeping	passive	in pain	inappropriate
anxious	abusive	afraid	upset
agitated			

APPLICATION:

Select client examples and describe specific behaviors which illustrate the following generalizations: Record your examples in the spaces provided.

1. Hostile

____

____

2. Combative

____

____

3. Confused

____

____

4. Disoriented

____

____

5. Cooperative

____

____

6. Uncooperative

____

____

7. Comfortable

____

____

8. In Pain

____

____

Organize logically. "I know what I want to say. I just can't get it down on paper" is a common complaint. The problem often arises from indecision about where to start and what to say next. If we know in advance what to say when, then we needn't waste time wondering what to say.

Two basic organizational modes are useful in documentation, time and importance. Perhaps the easiest way to organize is time, and many regulatory bodies and health care agencies mandate chronological order. To apply, simply record your observations and interventions in their order of occurrence. What happened first? Second? Next? Be sure to label each entry with a specific time reference. Avoid block entries which attempt to cover stretches of time. For example, label an entry 8:15 but not 8:15-9:30, and then record observations as soon as possible after they occur.

In addition, weigh the importance of your observations and interventions, and place the most important first, especially if they provide a frame of reference for the reader. For example, labored breathing and chest pain during exercise are more important than the presence of stiffness during exercise. The breathing difficulty is life threatening and provides a context for other observations.

Group related bits of information. For example, cluster discussion of diet related items or observations of skin condition. Don't jump from diet to skin and back to diet.

Finally, while including routine data which already appear on flow charts or graphs is unnecessary, emphasizing critical observations by reinforcing them in your notes is a good idea. For example, if the client's pulse fluctuates widely, be sure to highlight the observation in the progress notes.

Information which is presented in logically organized clusters of like ideas is easy to read and comprehend. Randomly arranged information requires the reader to rearrange, and interpret, and thus waste time.

Write objectively. You are a reporter, not a commentator. Opinions are interesting in cocktail party conversations, but don't belong in the medical record. Judgmental language is misleading and can hamper communication. For example, to say that a client is "manipulative" is merely to express an opinion. Write instead that the client "refuses medications unless she gets a kiss." Use this approach rather than generalized labels which convey only your attitude.

In addition, use direct quotes of the client's comments to convey the client's attitude or condition. Be sure to place quotation marks around key words attributed to the client.

"Good" and "normal" are common judgments. Substitute the observations which lead to your conclusions. "Good" may mean "pain-free" or "not infected;" "normal" may mean "not hemorrhaging" or "blemish free." Similarly, "well," "poorly," and "within normal limits" say nothing.

Judgment terms color the perception of your reader and may influence the reader's objectivity, thus influencing the quality of care.

APPLICATION:

Use the spaces provided to replace the judgment below with examples of specific observations. Quote sample client statements where possible.

1. IVAC infusing well.

 ____

 ____

2. Appetite good.

 ____

 ____

3. Appetite poor.

 ____

 ____

4. ROM (Range of Motion) normal.

 ____

 ____

5. Client tolerates procedure well.

 ____

 ____

APPLICATION continued.

6. Client had a comfortable night.

____

____

7. Client understands instruction.

____

____

Present accessibly. Information which is easy to read is easy to understand. Concentrate on short sentences, using capitals and periods. Cluster like items and shift to a new line when you shift ideas. Line out blank spaces. Avoid stringing ideas together with commas and dashes: these marks will obscure your message. Dashes, slashes, and commas are interrupters but not terminal points. Never use ditto marks.

The following example is difficult to read:

12-28-8-; 8 P.	Taught self administration on nph insulin—client demonstrated insulin injection according to protocol, did independently, no cues—taught urine testing for sugar and acetone—client demonstrated procedure according to protocol—did independently—no cues—dietitian instructed in 1500 cal. ADA diet. M. Washington, R.N.

This example is easier to read and understand:

12-28-8-; 8 P. Taught self administration NPH insulin.
Client demonstrated administration according to protocol independently.
Taught urine testing for sugar and acetone.
Client demonstrated procedure according to protocol independently.
Dietitian instructed client in 1500 cal. ADA diet.
M. Washington, R.N.

Omit subjects, verbs, and prepositions which are obvious or grammatically understood as long as clarity doesn't suffer; in the example above, client shows the shift in subject and is necessary for clarity.

Proofread. Sometimes the best way to save time is to spend time. Take a minute to proofread, since an omission can garble your message and waste your reader's time. Omissions are a common error: If you need to put in an omitted word, use a caret, like this: "Put in omitted word." Be sure to initial the addition and sign each entry with your name and title. Always use permanent ink, never pencil.

If you must delete an unnecessary word or idea, draw a line through like this: "Delete a ~~word~~ word ~~like~~ like this." Be sure the deleted word is still readable and be sure to initial the deletion. Writing "error" is unnecessary, though many regulatory bodies require it.

Fix misspellings which could confuse or mislead. Either delete and replace or correct. For example, "interdermal" could be corrected "interdermal." Never "white out" an entry.

Few health care agencies use the standard printer's marks shown above; follow the policy of your institution. Where no policy exists, the standard marks may be useful.

Formats

Two styles of formats are current in documenting client care: SOAP notes and narrative notes. The narrative note is the traditional "source oriented" note; the SOAP note is "problem oriented." The guidelines presented in this chapter apply to both.

How SOAP works. SOAP notes are a part of the overall scheme of the Problem Oriented Medical Records system. The SOAP format prescribes four focal points for discussing the client: Subjective, Objective, Assessment, and Plan. These four points present a system that assists the practitioner in identifying and dealing with client problems. The chart below illustrates the way SOAP sections should work:

Subjective:	Record what the client, client's family, or a significant other says about the problem.
Objective:	Record your observations.
Assessment:	Explain the status of the problem.
Plan:	Report the interventions you intend.

Each SOAP entry refers to a specific problem taken from the client's master problem list. Notes on the client's chart use the numbers on the problem list. If your agency doesn't use the problem list, simply state the problem you are addressing. Here are some samples:

Examples:

Nurse's Note

Problem #3: Alteration in body temperature: fever of unknown origin.

1-19-8-; 1:02 P.

S: "I don't feel as hot as I did earlier today, but I am sweating."

O: T 100^{4}; P 88; R 18. Skin warm; diaphoretic. Face pink, less flushed than at 4 P.

A: Temperature has decreased during past 24 h.

P:
1. Monitor TPR $\bar{q}$ 2h.
2. Increase fluids to minimum of 1000 cc/8 h.
3. Teach client to report signs indicating increase in temperature: chills, increased warmth.
4. Report temp. > 101° to physician on call.

D. Adkins, L.P.N.

Social Work Note

Problem #7: Client disposition

3-18-8-; 2 P.

S: (oldest daughter) ''Why is my mother being moved? I just don't understand! She'll die if she leaves here!''

O: Daughter flinging her arms, screaming, and crying in response to the hospital's decision to transfer her mother, Mrs. P. Mrs. P. has been a patient for 11 yrs, but has had no intensive therapy during the past 5 yrs. Needs a nursing home or extended care facility rather than a rehabilitation setting.

A: Oldest daughter believes that moving Mrs. P. will cause severe depression and a lack of will to live.

P:
1. Assure the oldest daughter that no transfer will occur for 2-3 months.
2. Talk with Mrs. P. about her feelings concerning possible transfer.
3. Plan a family conference next week with all three daughters, the physician, the head nurse, and the social worker to discuss alternatives for Mrs. P.
4. Discuss the outcome of the family conference with Mrs. P.

Cheryl Johnson, M.S.W.

Dietary Note

Problem #4: Lack of knowledge of 2 Gm Na^+ diet

3-18-8-; 3 P.

S: "I don't know the difference between a 2 Gram, 4 Gram, or whatever Gram diet. Is sodium the same thing as salt?"

O: Has had difficulty selecting appropriate foods for a 2 Gm Na^+ restriction. B/P has not been controlled by diet at home before this admission.

A: Although taught about his diet 6 months ago client cannot explain how to develop a 2 Gm Na^+ meal plan.

P:
1. Begin the teaching concerning his diet with the assumption that he knows nothing about it.
2. Meet with and teach his wife about the diet.
3. Provide written literature, including a list of high salt foods and several sample menus.
4. Have client select foods for a one-day meal plan.

Kay Morris, R.D.

Occupational Therapy Note

Problem #1: Dependence in dressing upper extremities

4-18-8-; 9 A.

S: "I'm having trouble putting on my blouse."

O: Sixty-two year old female had (R) CVA three weeks ago. Can dress lower extremities without assistance, but has difficulty with placement of unaffected arm into blouse sleeve. States the steps in the dressing procedure correctly.

A: Independent in dressing except for U. E. Needs less restrictive blouses or sweaters to facilitate U. E. dressing.

P:
1. Have daughter bring in larger blouses (at least one size larger).
2. Try overhead method of U. E. dressing.
3. Practice dressing techniques on unit and in department.

Jan Evans, O.T.R.

Variants on SOAP include SOAPIE and SOAPIER, the exact format depending on agency policy. The additional letters stand for:

Implementation: Record which parts of the plan you actually perform.

Evaluation: Report the effectiveness of the steps taken.

Revision: Revise the original plan based on your evaluation.

Generally, IER entries occur after SOAP entries as follow-on. The note above might continue:

Example:
Problem #3: Fever

1-20-8-; 12:30 A.	I:	1. TPR monitored. 2. Fluids increased to 1000 cc. 3. Ct. taught to report signs of increased temp.
	E:	T = 99.6; P = 76; R = 16.
	R:	1. Monitor TPR $\bar{q}$ 4 h. 2. Record I & O. J. Salamone, R.N.

While SOAPIE and SOAPIER formats may seem redundant, they do require users to carry out and document all the elements of assessment, planning, implementation, and evaluation.

How narrative works. Narrative notes should also document all of these elements. Since the narrative format is less formal, however, it provides no stimulus to remind the writer what to include. The writer must develop a mental checklist to assist in preparing the notes. The SOAPIER notes above rendered in narrative form might look like this:

1-19-8-; 10 P.	T 100.4; P 88; R 18. Skin warm; diaphoretic. Face pink, less flushed than at 4 P. States "I don't feel as hot as I did earlier today, but I am sweating." D. Adkins, L.P.N.
1-20-8-; 12:30 A.	T 99.6; P 76; R 16. Fluid intake 1000 cc since 4 P. Taught to report signs of temp. increase. J. Salamone, R.N.

In this case, the P and R data would appear in the client's care plan rather than in the progress notes. Users of the SOAP variants would be required to write these data twice unless the care plan form excludes the action plan column, as some agency's forms now do. Clearly, an advantage of the SOAP variants is that they display all the elements in one place.

Advantages and disadvantages. The format you use will depend on your agency's policy. Both SOAP and narrative have strengths and weakneses. The best way to approach their use is to adapt them to the requirements of your situation.

Each style offers advantages and disadvantages. The SOAP format offers formal structure which guides the writer, causing focus on specific client problems in an organized manner. SOAP may be somewhat inflexible in that sometimes data are difficult to fit into the focal points, but the focusing helps eliminate meaningless data.

The narrative form is less structured and formal, thus more flexible. Narrative notes tend to synthesize varied data into one complete client picture. Each SOAP note represents only a part of that picture.

Effective Charting Do's and Don'ts

Do

1. State observable facts.
2. Record all elements of the problem solving/assessment process.
3. Give a picture of physical, spiritual, and psychosocial condition and progress of client.
4. Record client statements related to condition using his/her own words whenever possible.
5. Include refusals of, or omissions in, care, treatments, or medications with reason for refusal or omission.
6. Chart accidents and unusual happenings promptly and honestly.
7. Include routine data in graphs or flow sheets whenever possible.
8. Present data in language and format which is:
   - Clear;
   - Accurate, complete, and pertinent;
   - Vivid;
   - Brief and concise;
   - Concrete and specific;
   - Neat and legible.

9. Make entries in sequence of events, being sure to date and time each entry. Begin entries with the most important data.
10. Line out white space.
11. Omit unnecessary words by using verb phrases when subject is clear.
12. Omit "client" or "patient" unless absolutely necessary to make meaning clear.
13. Use professional standard terminology and agency approved standard abbreviations only.
14. Separate statements with periods for clarity and neatness and begin each statement with a capital letter.
15. Sign all entries with written signature and title.
16. Record notes promptly.
17. Use permanent ink to make all entries.
18. Proofread.
19. Make corrections neatly by drawing a single line through the error. Initial corrections.

Don't

1. Express opinions, value judgments, or conclusions.
2. "Block" chart.
3. Skip lines between entries.
4. Use ditto marks.
5. Print signature.
6. Chart before the fact.
7. Erase or "whiteout" a chart notation.

Exercises

Rewrite, reorganize, and correct, the progress notes below. Use narrative or SOAP format, depending on your agency's format.

Exercise 1

2/23/8-	6:30 P Admitted to floor via stretcher accompanied by daughter, appears weak and slightly confused, pt. did not know his doctor who has been seeing him on a constant basis. Daughter states that pt. has been eating much for the past two weeks. He becomes confused by night and wanders around RN
	7:30 P Had a 1/4 cup of coffee with much persuasion. RN
	10 P Pt is congested but unable to produce any sputum. Medicated with Motrin for muscle pain. RN
2/14/8-	7 A daughter with patient through night, no C/O, slept all night, incontinent. RN
	7 A-12 N Bedrest maintained—Complete AM care given—Positioned from side to side. Appetite poor. Taking fluids fair—Inc. of urine. Down to x-ray for chest film. Pt. seems confused at times. Tried to get out of bed. Lower bed rails ordered. RN

Exercise 2

2/18/8-

7 P 72 y/o w/m—obese admitted to Dr. A's service with DX deep phlebitis L leg. L leg swollen, red and warm from thigh to toes. In bed with L leg on pillow. Medical hx includes glaucoma, heart condition with fluid retention, bilat hearing difficulties with hearing device R ear. States NKA, pt. takes Lasix ī day, K-Lyte ī day, Erythromycin q̄ 6°, Zomax,—dosages unknown—taken today however. Also Timotic 0.5% ī gtt. o.u. q̄ 12° & Pilocar 2% ī gtt. o.u. q 6°. Poss s. q. heparin also. Surgical history includes T & A as child. VSS - BP 158/76. CCU for U/A sent to lab.

RN

9 P P.A. in to talk with pt. Eye gtts given. IV started 1 liter D/5W with 20,000 Units heparin on IVAC #15.

RN

2/19/8-

7 A c/o getting no sleep. IVAC infusing well. Eye gtts given.

RN

9 A AM care by bedside. Legs elevated L leg grossly edematous and warm to touch. Nonproductive cough. IVs of D5W with 20,000 units. heparin infusing well.

RN

11 A Afebrile. Sleeps periodically. States he did not rest well last night.

RN

11:30 A Visiting with wife.

RN

3 P Large amount of diarrheal stool. Lomotil ī tab given.

RN

Exercise 3

12/22/8- 1 P Pt. admitted to Rm. 207W via wheelchair under service of Dr. H. from rheumatology clinic. Pt. has bilateral foot ulcers—was using Neosporin powder on ulcers at home. Pt. diabetic—takes NPH insulin 40 Units in AM and 22 in PM. Pt. has 11 year history of scleroderma. Pt. also has history of bronchitis—uses O_2 at home prn.

RN

9 P To x-ray via wheelchair, needs ccu, resting in bed without discomfort.

RN

10 P Bed cradle removed because it falls off easily and pt. worried that it may hit her foot. c/o cold feet with pain, medicated with Darvocet N 100, VSS.

RN

11 P c/o severe foot pain, medicated with Tylox po, refused NPH insulin states that she is allergic to it, blood sugar 103, Dr. W. aware of pt. not receiving insulin.

RN

6 A Slept poorly, c/o much discomfort, med with minimal relief. Dalmane given for sleep with affect, afebrile-pillows positioned at ft. of bed to prevent covers from hitting feet, not utilizing O_2 at present.

LPN

1/25/8- 4:20 A Quiet night, med with Tylox tab po @ 12:30 AM for pain. Drg @ 3 AM Done @ Rx. Pt. states "I don't see what else can be done for this toe (looking @ R greater toe ulcer), they might as well take it off, I lost the battle." Pt. reassured as much as possible. N/C of pain at this time.

LPN

7 A-3 P Much more comfortable day—Complains of less pain—Rx to feet done as ordered. VSS—Appetite continues poor—Has not voided this tour.

LPN

3 P-7 P Quiet afternoon with complaints of pain. Has remained in bed. Refused Tylox at 6 PM.

LPN

Exercise 4

Mrs. W., 27, was admitted two days ago for an emergency cholecystectomy. Today you are assigned to care for her during the 7-3 shift. Her orders are:

IV D5/1/2 NS @ 125 cc hr.,
Keflin Gm ī q̄ 4 h IVMB,
Demerol 75 mg c̄ Vistaril
25 mg IM q̄ 4 h prn pain,
NPO,
V/S q̄ 4 h,
Incentive spirometer q̄ 2 h,
Deep Breathe with Cough q̄ h,
I+O.

When checking her dressing, you note that her abdomen is taut and distended; bowel sounds are absent. She reports generalized abdominal discomfort, particularly on light palpation. Her abdominal dressing is dry and intact. Vitals are 101°-100-22, B/P 130/78 @ 10 am.

She has a productive cough with copious amounts of whitish, foamy sputum. You report your findings to the physician, after giving her prn pain medication.

Write two sets of progress notes which specify her care during your shift, given that you carry out all of the above orders. One set will be narrative format, the other SOAP (IER).

Exercise 5

Mrs. H., 64, 195 lbs., 5′4″, was admitted last evening to your unit with cellulitis of her (R) foot and a 30 year history of diabetes mellitus. Five months ago she removed a callous from her foot with a razor blade. She did not notify her physician.

Her admission orders include:

NPH insulin 15 u. s.c. q̄ AM,
Gentamycin 80 mg q̄ 8 h IVMB,
Synthroid 0.1 mg q̄ AM (for 15 yr. hx of hypothyroidism),
Standard wound precautions.
Bedrest c̄ (R) leg↑,
1500 cal ADA diet,
Betadine soaks q̄ shift to (R) foot,
Wet to Dry Betadine dressing to wound on (R) foot q̄ shift,
V/S q̄ 4 h.

You are assigned to care for Mrs. H. during the 7-3 shift. While changing her dressing @ 10 am you notice that she frowns and closes her eyes. The wound on her (R) foot is located over the first metatarsal joint. It is an open area 1/4″ deep, 1/2″ in diameter, and is draining yellowish, purulent material with a foul odor (amount difficult to determine as it blends c̄ Betadine). Whitish-yellow tissue is visible throughout the wound. Her V/S at 10 am are 100^{6}-96-24, B/P 150/94.

Write two sets of progress notes which specify her care during your shift, given that you carry out all of the above orders. One set will be narrative format, the other SOAP (IER).

Chapter 2
Writing Client Assessments

Objectives

After reading this chapter and completing the exercises, you should be able to write client assessments.

Specifically, in this chapter you learn to:

- Identify guidelines for assessing clients.
- Identify formats used for recording assessment data.
- Evaluate sample assessment forms.
- Identify skills used for client interviews.
- Apply procedures for client interviews.

The quality of the written assessment data depends in part on the quality of the information to be recorded. Thoroughness and accuracy in performing your assessment is critical.

Assessment is a continuous, systematic method of data collection which provides the basis for analyzing client problems. Assessment is a three-part process: data collection, data analysis, data recording.

In this chapter, we will discuss:

1. Who should assess.
2. When to assess.
3. What to assess.
4. Where to assess.
5. How to assess.
6. How to write an assessment.

Who Should Assess

The assessment process is an integral part of each health professional's practice. Nurses, social workers, physical therapists, occupational therapists, respiratory therapists, and dietitians can provide adequate and effective care only when the client's problems are accurately identified. Problem identification follows from the data collected.

In a sense, assessment is analogous to the data collection step of the scientific process for problem solving: collect all available pertinent data; identify actual and potential problems; and implement planned steps to solve the identified problems.

Ideally, all members of the health team collaborate to share data related to their respective disciplines and validate findings with each other. Whenever possible, they also validate their findings with the client before preparing the comprehensive care plan.

When to Assess

The assessment process occurs continuously, beginning on admission or initial health care visit, on a daily basis, and at the time of client discharge from hospital, clinic, or home care. While the client is usually the main source for information, family members and significant others are also valuable resources. For example, the latter sources are particularly useful when the client is disoriented, comatose, very young, nonverbal, or otherwise unable to communicate.

In addition, assessing the client's home environment and community may be helpful. An arthritic client, for instance, may not be able to perform activities for daily living if structural barriers exist at home. Alterations or adaptations may be necessary for achieving functional independence.

What to Assess

Each care profession collects its own type of data on the client. Social workers, for example, need information describing the financial, vocational, educational, and social status of the client. A thorough social worker also considers the client's history and current physical condition. Each professional should regard the client as a whole being, concurrently assessing physical, psychological, and social domains.

The focus of a nursing assessment is perhaps broader than that of other health professionals. Although other professionals ***consider*** bio-psychosocial data, they tend to concentrate on one of these areas, such as social status and needs. By contrast, a nursing assessment includes the comprehensive collection of data in all three domains.

Assessment data is organized into two major components: history and physical assessment. Perhaps mislabeled, a ''history'' not only includes prior events and experiences, but also displays current client status. Certain types of information are useful in a nursing history:

1. Experience with illness and hospitalization and its significance to the individual.
2. Level of knowledge about and understanding of the health problem, diagnosis, and therapeutic regimen.
3. Occupational and social roles.
4. Educational and intellectual capacity.
5. Recreational, religious, and usual health practices.
6. Language usage.
7. Economic status and employment patterns.
8. Level of behavioral growth and development.
9. Current and past coping behaviors used for handling stress.
10. Usual cultural patterns of daily living, such as food preferences, hygiene and sleep patterns, and elimination routines, as well as interfamily relationships and lifestyle.

11. Relationships with others, particularly those who are "significant," those who influence the life and decisions of the client.

The emphasis on health practices and stress adaptation has been unique to the nursing profession, but other disciplines are recognizing the need to collect data in these areas for a more comprehensive approach to client management.

The second component, physical assessment, is sometimes considered to be solely within the realm of medical practice. Unlike the physician's physical ***examination*** however, physical ***assessment*** does not lead to a medical diagnosis. Rather it highlights, or "flags," areas of deviation from the "norm" and enables the health professional to anticipate actual or potential client problems.

Physical assessment includes a thorough description of the health problem which has motivated the client to seek health care and an evaluation of each body system.

Here we have discussed history and physical assessment separately; however, they generally appear together in the assessment record. Some professions and agencies prefer an integrated approach, where history and physical data appear together, grouped by body system or other systematic scheme. As long as the reader can understand the information, the method of presentation is optional.

Where to Assess

Assessment is not restricted to clients in a hospital setting. Professionals employed in physicians' offices, outpatient clinics, community health centers, and home health care need to assess their clients. The initial assessment or data base develops immediately following client-professional introduction. The process need not be lengthy, but must be comprehensive.

Each agency develops its own forms or specifies locations whereon to record assessment data. The data record must be placed in an accessible, clearly marked location. Frequently, the assessment record ends up at the back of a client's chart where it is misplaced or never used. The valuable time spent in data collection is wasted, and worse, the client's plan of care is not complete or is based on the wrong information.

How to Assess

Now that the who, when, what, and where questions are answered, the remaining question is "How do I get started?"

Most agencies have designated assessment forms for recording data. Regardless of type, the form serves simply as a guide for data collection which helps to organize data, but is not, in and of itself, an exhaustive tool.

Traditionally, health professionals have recorded data in a narrative format on the progress note records. Often the information could not be easily extracted, as pertinent data were buried in a mass of unrelated, unnecessary information.

Assessment Formats

More recently a variety of forms have appeared to capture pertinent assessment data. Basically, three types of data base formats are available: structured, semistructured, and unstructured. Each has advantages and disadvantages.

Structured. The structured format frequently appears as a checklist in which the assessor can check whether or not a listed item is present, or respond in a "yes or no" manner. Below is an example of a structured format:

Abdomen (Mark "✓" if present)

Scars	________	Masses	________
Bruises	________	Bowel sounds	________
Swelling	________		
Tenderness	________		

The major advantages of the structured tool are easy use and time savings. A drawback, however, is the lack of space in which to record additional information and the subsequent restriction of the assessor's creativity.

Semi-structured. The second type, or semi-structured format, allows for additional comments and open statement responses, while structuring basic, routine information for brevity. The closed statements provide cues for the professional, but permit flexibility when elaborating important findings. An example follows:

Upper extremities:

Right Strength:

Sensation:

Range of Motion:

The blank space also provides an area where the assessor can sketch diagrams and draw scales which will clearly illustrate the findings.

Unstructured. The open, or unstructured format, provides fewer cues and looks similar to that used by physicians. Such a tool is often difficult to use when the desired goal is a comprehensive assessment. On the other hand, an unstructured tool might be particularly useful for a more narrowly focused assessment, such as that needed by respiratory therapists. The form might look like this.

Respiratory Therapy Assessment

Client ________ Age Sex

Date ______

Respiratory Status: (Lung fields):

Cardiac Status: (from Physician's History and Physical):

APPLICATION

Answer the items below regarding assessment formats:

1. List one advantage and one disadvantage of a structured assessment format.

   ____

   ____

2. List one advantage and one disadvantage of an open or unstructured assessment format.

   ____

   ____

Observation and Interview

Regardless of format chosen, the "how-to" of assessment is the same. Use two techniques, observation and interview, to collect data. Observation is not only a part of physical assessment, but is also much more.

During the entire assessment process you should be observing and recording nonverbal client behavior. These data provide clues to physical and psychosocial problems. For example, a client's verbal denial of chest pain may be accompanied by grimacing or a loss of eye contact with the interviewer. Record both verbal and nonverbal responses.

In addition to observation skills, a thorough assessment requires a host of communication skills to interview the client. The formal interview is purposeful and structured to conserve time and energy for both the client and interviewer.

The assessment interview has several purposes. The most obvious purpose is to gather information about the client that will enable the health care team to develop a plan of care. Utilizing a data base form as a guide only, interview the client on initial encounter.

Choose the time for interview carefully. Eliminate the possibility of interruption by phone calls, visitors, or other distractions. If the client is not in a private room or quiet area, find a place conducive to conversation and free of distractions.

Determine the client's physical, mental, and emotional condition prior to the intended interview. A client in pain, for example, is not likely to answer questions or discuss any health care needs besides pain. An anxious client is not likely to give complete answers or listen intently to the interviewer.

In addition to timeliness, consider differences in age, culture, and ethnic backgrounds between client and health professional. Don't condemn or mock a client for health care beliefs or practices.

Once you've decided that the time is right for the inteview, introduce yourself. Ask the client what name the staff should use; otherwise, use last name only.

Now, begin the interview. Don't read the questions or statements listed on the form from beginning to end. Instead, allow the client to talk freely, even if it means that you have to skip from one area of the form to another. If your client begins to ramble, get "back on track" by asking direct pertinent questions or using cues: "What about . . .?" "Do you mean . . .?" Most importantly, focus on relevant client concerns. Active client participation in the assessment process is your goal.

In addition to collecting data, then, the interview allows the client to ventilate. Again, you need sound communication skills. Don't offer false reassurance; be supportive and listen. Due to time limitations, you might spend most of your interview asking questions but little time listening. Both processes are vital for an adequate assessment.

The assessment interview offers an excellent opportunity for esablishing a professional-client relationship. The client begins to trust the care provider, forming the basis for future interactions.

Once the data have been collected and the interpersonal relationship established, validate the information with the client. Make sure you've obtained a complete picture that is accurate. An experienced interviewer can conduct an assessment interview and validate the data collected in 20 to 30 minutes.

Although most of our discussion here centers around the admission interview, interviews are conducted on discharge of the client from a hospital, clinic, or home care. Again, a variety of forms are available for documentation depending on the agency's policies and procedures. In any event, the discharge assessment, or summary, should present as thorough a picture as the initial data base.

How to Write An Assessment

The guidelines for writing an assessment are very similar to those for writing progress notes, outlined in Chapter 1. As in progress notes, report observations in concrete, sensual language. For example, "complains of sharp, stabbing, intermittent pain in right upper abdominal quadrant" is much more useful than "complains of abdominal pain." In the latter statement regarding the client's pain, we are left with many questions about the sensation and exact location of the pain.

Include all of the information you think might be important, but report it clearly and concisely. Wordiness prevents the reader from extracting the significant data; lack of meaningful detail presents an incomplete picture of the client's status.

Avoid using generalizations such as "cooperative" and "depressed." Include behaviors which support your judgments in the assessment, not useless and unsubtantial labels. Also, avoid the terms "normal" or "abnormal." What is <u>normal</u> to one client may be <u>abnormal</u> for another. For example, a blood pressure 90/50 may be usual for a young, athletic client, but not sufficient for an elderly, obese, client. Record the actual data rather than a judgment of normalcy.

"Appears" and "seems" are similarly vague terms, making your reader suspect you're unsure of your assessment data. Report your data in concrete, observable language that appeals directly to the senses.

When your assessment data are collected, organize by body system or other scheme designated by your agency's policies and assessment format. Within each component of the assessment, body system or otherwise, display data in a logical, ordered manner. Record significant information first to bring the data to the reader's attention immediately. For example, inspiratory wheezing indicates pathology and should appear early in the respiratory assessment.

Group related pieces of information. Group all data regarding breath sounds, and similarly group data on inspection of the chest. The assessment data, then, are logically organized for accessibility to the reader.

The assessment form used in your facility dictates the presentation of data. Oftentimes, space is limited, sacrificing completeness of information. Some writers use non-standard abbreviations in a space-saving effort. Rather than risking incompleteness or jeopardizing understanding by the reader, use additional paper to record the data. Progress note forms can be used for this purpose. Remember, even though <u>you</u> may understand what you wrote, others may not.

The following example of an unstructured abdominal assessment illustrates the guidelines we've highlighted.

<u>Client</u>: G.W. <u>Age</u>: 74 <u>Sex</u>: F

<u>Abdominal Assessment</u>:

<u>History</u>: C/O obstipation × 7 days before admission.
<u>Physical</u>: Distended, taut, shiny skin.
<u>Findings</u>: Midline scar—umbilicus to pubis.
Tenderness—LUQ + LLQ.
Tympany—all quadrants.
Hypoactive BS – LUQ + LLQ (0-1/min.).
Hyperactive BS – RUQ + RLQ (10-12/min.).

Note that the physical data are presented in linear, outline form for optimum readability. Inspection, palpation, percussion, and auscultation findings appear in that order. In addition to physical findings, information regarding pertinent related history is also included.

APPLICATION:

1. Using the inspection, palpation, percussion, and auscultation ordering listed above in the abdominal assessment, write a respiratory physical assessment for a typical client with asthma.

2. List questions you would ask and observations you would make for a client in pain.

The following terms may be useful to assist a client in describing pain:

dull	sharp
stabbing	continuous
intermittent	vise-like
crushing	burning
stinging	tingling

The Next Step

After having collected data, analyze your findings. Look for information suggesting actual or potential client health problems. Consider physical, psychological, and social data during your analysis.

Five sources provide information for problem identification:

Observable data.
Physical findings reported by the laboratory
or similar source.
Client reports.
Family reports.
Client history.

Record information on your agency's assessment form using the following guidelines, adapted as necessary to your agency's policy. Each health professional uses the assessment form specifically designed for that profession.

Observable data: State signs and symptoms present sepcifically and concretely. Use the clearest, most concise terms available. Use language that appeals to the senses; for example, "purulent, draining, sacral decubitus, 1 in. diameter, 1/4 in. deep" or "deep tendon reflexes, left leg, 3+."

Physical findings: Select deviations which reinforce the assessment. For example, use results of electromyography to confirm decreased muscle activity.

Client reports: Record client comments directly. Use the client's exact words whenever possible, selecting key words to illustrate the findings. Elicit specific information regarding location, frequency, intensity, and duration of the problem. Use quotation marks to indicate direct quotes. For example: "Client reports 'Continuous, dull ache in left shoulder,' pointing to anterior joint."

Family reports: Elicit information from family members or significant others both to complement and to expand the assessment. Confirm suspected alcoholism by questioning, for example. Having observed tremens and signs of disorientation, seek additional information. Use the individual's exact words whenever possible: "Brother reports client has been drinking 'a pint of gin a day for ten years'."

Client history: Identify aspects which relate directly to the assessment. When in doubt, include items of questionable relevance. For example, a parent's or sibling's having been hypertensive might not seem to bear directly on the client's condition but should be noted.

Assessment Guidelines

Keep the following points in mind when assessing your client:

1. Use the comprehensive, systematic approach to data collection.
2. Assess your client on admission and analyze the data collected.
3. Include client history and physical assessment data in the data base.
4. Interview your client at an appropriate and convenient time.
5. Structure the interview, but don't restrict the client's responses if pertinent.
6. Validate your findings with the client and other health care professionals, if possible.

Exercises

Exercise 1

Using the following blank assessment form, interview a client or peer using the guidelines specified in the chapter.

Exercise 2

a. Review the following completed data base (pp. 46–47) and list its strengths and weaknesses below:

Strengths	Weaknesses

b. Revise the data base to ensure accuracy and completeness.

City Hospital
Nursing Admission
Side 1

Date ____________ Time ____________ Admitted by ____________

REASON FOR PRESENT ADMISSION ____________

ADMITTED FROM

( ) ER
( ) Work
( ) Home
( ) Dr. Office
( ) Other ____________

ALLERGIES

Drugs ____________

Foods ____________

Environment ____________

MODE OF ADMISSION

( ) Ambulatory
( ) Wheelchair
( ) Stretcher

PHYSICIAN/RESIDENT NOTIFIED

Name ____________
Time ____________

VITAL SIGNS

Temp. ____________ ( ) Oral ( ) Rectal ( ) Auxillary

Pulse ____________ ( ) Radial ( ) Apical ( ) Regular ( ) Irregular

Resp. ____________ ( ) Regular ( ) Irregular ( ) Labored

B/P ____________

Ht. ______ Wt. ______

EXPLANATION TO PATIENT

( ) Call system
( ) Electric bed
( ) ID band
( ) Admission kit
( ) Visiting hours
( ) Meal times
( ) Bathroom
( ) Smoking regulations
( ) Television
( ) Telephone
( ) Patient's Bill of Rights

PROSTHESIS OR DEVICES

( ) Dentures
( ) Upper ( ) Lower ( ) Partial
( ) Eyeglasses
( ) Contact lenses
( ) Hearing aid
( ) Braces type ____________
( ) Cane
( ) Walker
( ) Crutches
( ) Other ____________

CURRENT MEDICATIONS (including PRN'S) ( ) none

Name	Dose	Route	Frequency	Time of last dose	With Pt.	Sent home	

NURSING ADMISSION

Side 2

HISTORY

Known Health Problems ( ) No

( ) Cancer
( ) Cataracts
( ) Diabetes
( ) Seizures
( ) Glaucoma
( ) Heart Disease
( ) High blood pressure
( ) Kidney disease
( ) Liver disease
( ) TB
( ) Chronic lung disease
( ) Other ______

PHYSICAL LIMITATIONS

( ) No

( ) Vision
( ) Hearing
( ) Speech
( ) Paralysis/paresis
( ) Amputation

( ) Other ______

PERSONAL HABITS

Bowel
Frequency ______
Last BM ______
Problem ______

Bladder
Frequency ______
Last Voiding ______
Problem ______

Diet at home ______

Tobacco ( ) yes ( ) no
Amount ______

Alcohol ( ) yes ( ) no
Amount ______

Other ______

GENERAL APPEARANCE

Skin Condition

( ) Warm
( ) Cold
( ) Dry
( ) Clammy
( ) Diaphoretic
( ) Edema Where? ______
( ) Reddened Where? ______
( ) Decubitus
(if so chart initiated)
( ) Other ______

Skin Color

( ) Pink
( ) Pale
( ) Cyanotic
( ) Mottled
( ) Other
______

Level of Consciousness

( ) Alert
( ) Lethargic
( ) Responds to voice
( ) Responds to pain
( ) Oriented
( ) Disoriented
( ) No response

OTHER OBSERVATIONS

______

CITY HOSPITAL
NURSING ADMISSION
Side 1

Date 10/3 Time 1 PM Admitted by S. Jones, R.N

REASON FOR PRESENT ADMISSION

Surgery

ADMITTED FROM

( ) ER
( ) Work
( ) Home
( ) Dr. Office
( ) Other ____

Came c̄ wife

ALLERGIES

Drugs ____

Foods ____

Environment pollen

MODE OF ADMISSION

( ) Ambulatory
( ) Wheelchair
( ) Stretcher

PHYSICIAN/RESIDENT NOTIFIED

Name Smith
Time 1:30 PM

VITAL SIGNS

Temp 98 ( ) Oral ( ) Rectal ( ) Auxillary

Pulse 82 ( ) Radial ( ) Apical ( ) Regular ( ) Irregular

Resp. 16 ( ) Regular ( ) Irregular ( ) Labored

B/P 118/94

Ht. ____ Wt. 165

EXPLANATION TO PATIENT

( ) Call system
( ) Electric bed
(✓) ID band
(✓) Admission kit
( ) Visiting hours
( ) Meal times
( ) Bathroom
( ) Smoking regulations
( ) Television
( ) Telephone
( ) Patient's Bill of Rights

PROSTHESIS OR DEVICES

( ) Dentures
( ) Upper ( ) Lower ( ) Partial
( ) Eyeglasses
( ) Contact lenses
( ) Hearing aid
( ) Braces type ____
( ) Cane
( ) Walker
( ) Crutches
( ) Other ____

CURRENT MEDICATIONS (including PRN'S) ( ) none

Name	Dose	Route	Freq-uency	Time of last dose	With Pt.	Sent home
Maalox						
Dig						

Nursing Admission

Side 2

HISTORY

Known Health Problems ( ) No

( ) Cancer
( ) Cataracts
( ) Diabetes
( ) Seizures
( ) Glaucoma
( ) Heart Disease
( ) High blood pressure
( ) Kidney disease
( ) Liver disease
( ) TB
( ) Chronic lung disease
( ) Other *Back trouble*

PHYSICAL LIMITATIONS

(✓) No

( ) Vision
( ) Hearing
( ) Speech
( ) Paralysis/paresis
( ) Amputation

( ) Other ______

PERSONAL HABITS

Bowel
Frequency *q.o.d.*
Last BM ______
Problem ______

Bladder
Frequency ______
Last Voiding ______
Problem ______

Diet at home
Lo fat

Tobacco (✓) yes ( ) no
Amount *1½ pks.*

Alcohol (✓) yes ( ) no
Amount *Social drinker*

Other ______

GENERAL APPEARANCE

Skin Condition

(✓) Warm
( ) Cold
( ) Dry
( ) Clammy
( ) Diaphoretic
( ) Edema Where? ______
( ) Reddened Where? ______
( ) Decubitus
(if so chart initiated)
( ) Other ______

Skin Color

( ) Pink
( ) Pale
( ) Cyanotic
( ) Mottled
( ) Other
______

Level of Consciousness

(✓) Alert
( ) Lethargic
( ) Responds to voice
( ) Responds to pain
( ) Oriented
( ) Disoriented
( ) No response

OTHER OBSERVATIONS

Chapter 3
Preparing The Comprehensive Client Care Plan

Objectives

After reading this chapter and completing the exercises, you should be able to prepare a client care plan.

Specifically in this chapter you learn to:

- Identify the steps in developing the comprehensive care plan.
- Identify and apply specified guidelines for care plan preparation.
- Prepare a sample care plan.
- Revise and correct ineffective care plan elements.

The purpose of the comprehensive care plan is to guide each member of the health care team. The plan organizes care and establishes a basis for consistency among the members of the team. By providing direction, the plan facilitates efficient delivery of care. Given a clear, well developed plan, health professionals need not waste time wondering what to do next.

Within 24 hours of the client's admission, the team, which typically includes therapists, the dietitian, the social worker, as well as nurses, and nursing assistants, meets to initiate the care plan based on client assessment. The person responsible for initiating the plan is the nurse to whom the client is assigned: this individual could be a primary nurse, a staff nurse, a community nurse, or a team leader, depending on the system of nursing care delivery. Ideally, the physician should offer comments and suggestions, since this plan should complement the treatment plan.

Effective care planning involves a four part process:

1. Identifying client problems.
2. Setting goals.
3. Developing an action plan.
4. Building in a feedback mechanism.

Identifying Client Problems

Problem identification relies on assessment data. Using assessment data, the team members locate deviations between what the client's condition should be and actually is. The team members list and rank these deviations, or problems.

Two formats are currently used for stating problems: the traditional "nursing problem" format and the "nursing diagnosis" format. Neither is a medical diagnosis, a disease process or disorder statement. Either may be used for independent nursing interventions and either may be used to describe actual or potential conditions.

In the nursing problem format, the problem statement may not state causality, and the problem statement is often a sign, symptom, or behavior, such as fever, pain, or nausea.

In the nursing diagnosis format the statement should always include causality, sometimes expressed as "related to" a disease process, disorder, or behavior. For example, the nursing diagnosis statement might be "impaired physical mobility related to right hemiparesis" or "impairment of skin integrity related to laminectomy."

The Sixth National Conference on Nursing Diagnosis (1984) has adopted a set of over 50 standard diagnoses which are available for reference. The diagnoses adopted generally represent categories of client problems. In order to individualize, the practitioner adds the "related to" statement and defining characteristics.

Choice of format depends, of course, on agency policy and client situation. For the client with complex medical diagnoses, the nursing problem format might be easier to apply if causal interrelationships are difficult to discriminate. The nursing diagnosis format is likely to be more useful when causes of signs, symptoms, and behaviors are readily identifiable.

The trend is toward using the nursing diagnosis format because of the advantages of standardization, primarily for ease of communication and for potential computerization. However, clarity within your agency is ultimately important, so use internal consensus to establish sets of problem statements which everyone can undersand. Table 3-1 lists those nursing diagnoses accepted for clinical testing.

APPLICATION:
Refer to Care Plan 1 at the end of this chapter. List 2 client problems: state them in nursing diagnosis format first. Then state them in nursing problem format.

Nursing Diagnosis Format:

1. ______________________________

____

2. ______________________________

____

Nursing Problem Format:

1. ______________________________

____

2. ______________________________

____

Table 3-1

Approved Nursing Diagnoses
North American Nursing Diagnosis Association

April, 1984

Activity intolerance*
Activity intolerance, potential*
Airway clearance, ineffective
Anxiety*
Bowel elimination, alteration in: constipation
Bowel elimination, alteration in: diarrhea
Bowel elimination, alteration in: incontinence
Breathing pattern, ineffective
Cardiac output, alteration in: decreased
Comfort, alteration in: pain
Communication, impaired: verbal
Coping, family: potential for growth
Coping, ineffective family: compromised
Coping, ineffective family: disabling
Coping, ineffective individual
Diversional activity, deficit
Family process, alteration in*† (formerly Family dynamics)
Fear
Fluid volume, alteration in: excess*†
Fluid volume deficit, actual
Fluid volume deficit, potential
Gas exchange, impaired
Grieving, anticipatory
Grieving, dysfunctional
Health maintenance, alteration in*
Home maintenance management, impaired
Injury, potential for: (poisoning, potential for; suffocation, potential for; trauma, potential for)
Knowledge deficit (specify)
Mobility, impaired physical
Noncompliance (specify)
Nutrition, alteration in: less than body requirements
Nutrition, alteration in: more than body requirements
Nutrition, alteration in: potential for more than body requirements
Oral mucous membrane, alteration in*
Parenting, alteration in: actual
Parenting, alteration in: potential
Powerlessness*
Rape trauma syndrome
Self-care deficit: feeding, bathing/hygiene, dressing/grooming, toileting
Self-concept, disturbance in: body image, self-esteem, role performance, personal identity
Sensory-perceptual alteration: visual, auditory, kinesthetic, gustatory, tactile, olfactory
Sexual dysfunction
Skin integrity, impairment of: actual
Skin integrity, impairment of: potential
Sleep pattern disturbance
Social isolation*†
Spiritual distress (distress of the human spirit)
Thought processes, alteration in
Tissue perfusion, alteration in: cerebral, cardiopulmonary, renal, gastrointestinal, peripheral
Urinary elimination, alteration in patterns
Violence, potential for: self-directed or directed at others

*Addition from 1982 Conference
†Moves from TBD list

Setting Goals

Problem statements provide the focus for developing goals. Each requires at least one goal and possibly more. Depending on the client's needs, both short and long term goals may be necessary. In any case, the care planning form you use should include a column for client problems and a separate column for related goals.

State goals in clear, measurable, realistic terms. Use action verbs which state intended outcomes in observable performances. Focus on the client so that goals are stated in terms of client progress. While client oriented goals are generally preferable to practitioner oriented goals, client goals are difficult to write when client outcomes are hard to pin down. Since the purpose of goals is to provide direction for planning, goals which are sufficiently clear to do so are useful whether client oriented or not. Validate practitioner oriented goals with the client. Date the goals.

A client centered goal is the statement of an expected outcome. Many care plans label the goal column "expected outcome." The terms are interchangeable.

Typical client oriented goals might include:
- Temperature will stabilize below 100° within 48 hours.
- Will feed self with fork within one week.

Typical practitioner oriented goals might include:
- Social worker will coordinate nursing home placement at least one week prior to discharge.
- Nurse will prevent post-appendectomy shock for at least 24 hours.

Note that each goal contains ***who*** will do ***what*** by ***when.*** Be sure goal statements follow the who, what, when formula.

Avoid making global or overly specific statements. Global goals such as "Prevent infection" are too general to be useful since such statements are not measurable. Specific goals such as "Take and record vital signs every 4 hours" are action steps, and belong in the action plan rather than among the goals. A statement is too specific if it cannot be broken into smaller pieces.

Table 3-2 lists action verbs and descriptors to use and avoid when planning goals.

Table 3-2

Action verbs	**Descriptors of standards**
Use:	Use:
state	independently
list	unassisted
perform	by (a certain time)
name	within (specific) limits
demonstrate (steps in a procedure)	according to standard or protocol
label	
calculate	
measure	
describe in own words	
explain	
use	
apply	
compare	
design	
restate	
Avoid	Avoid
understanding	safely
demonstrate knowledge of	competently
recognize	accurately
appreciate	fully
remember	properly
recall	appropriately
accept	adequately
cope	sufficiently

APPLICATION:
In the spaces provided, rewrite the statements below as specific client centered goals. Be sure to include who does what by when.

1. Teach self care of foot wound.

____

____

2. Learn to brush teeth.

____

____

3. Restore ambulation.

____

____

4. Use the incentive spirometer.

____

____

5. Exercise.

____

____

6. Improve self image.

____

____

Developing the Action Plan

To develop the action plan, first list the steps needed to achieve each goal. Second, place the steps in order and check for completeness. Third, develop detail in steps as needed. Fourth, consider Murphy's Law. Display the plan for each goal in a separate column on the care plan form.

For example, the steps in the action plan for the goal "Nurse will prevent post-appendectomy shock for at least 24 hours" might be as follows. Note that each item begins with an action verb and has been fully developed, including breaking into substeps.

Take and record vital signs every 4 hours.
Assess pain level PRN.
Alleviate pain by:
- (a) providing hygiene,
- (b) repositioning,
- (c) giving medication as ordered.

Provide for adequate hydration by:
- (a) measuring and recording intake and output,
- (b) monitoring IV rate,
- (c) assessing skin condition,
- (d) monitoring temperature.

Assess surgical dressing for bleeding.
Perform abdominal assessment.

The verbs and descriptors listed in Table 3-2 would also be helpful in writing this plan.

Now review the steps and ask yourself if they are in the proper order. Use time and priority as organizing modes. Here, since complications can be potentially life threatening, priority order is preferable. Thus, the steps above might be organized this way; be sure to number them:

1. Assess surgical dressing for bleeding.
2. Take and record vital signs every 4 hours.
3. Perform abdominal assessment.
4. Provide for adequate hydration by:
   - (a) measuring and recording intake and output,
   - (b) monitoring IV rate,
   - (c) assessing skin condition,
   - (d) monitoring temperature.
5. Assess pain level PRN.
6. Alleviate pain by:
   - (a) giving medication as ordered.
   - (b) providing hygiene,
   - (c) repositioning.

Make sure to include all necessary steps. Ask yourself "Have I left out anything that should be done?"

Next, review each step for sufficient development. For example, step 4 includes a list of measures for providing adequate hydration. Don't assume that all team members know what to do unless your hospital has a standard protocol for this step. If a standard protocol is available, refer to it in the step.

Finally, consider Murphy's Law. Ask yourself "What could go wrong?" at each step. Then revise each step to prevent "whatever can go wrong" from going wrong. If preventing is impossible, build in action which will minimize the negative impact of whatever goes wrong. For example, since clients may deny pain because they don't want to take pain medication, step 5 could say. "Assess pain level PRN. Consider client's: (a) facial expression, (b) body position, (c) skin condition, (d) history of receptivity to pain medication, and (e) comments." In the absence of a standard protocol, considering Murphy's law is especially important.

APPLICATION:

Write a client centered goal below, based on an identified problem of a selected client. Prepare an action plan which addresses the goal. Use additional paper if needed.

Goal: ______________________________

____

Action Plan: ______________________________

____

____

____

____

____

____

____

____

____

____

____

____

____

Building in a Feedback Mechanism

Gathering feedback involves monitoring and evaluating the care plan and revising it when necessary. Include checkpoints in the goals and actions. For example, "Assess surgical dressing for bleeding at least hourly" specifies frequency and provides a monitoring system. "Perform abdominal assessment every 4 hours" does likewise. Monitor at predetermined intervals in order to evaluate progress. Record the steps on the action plan column of your care plan form after sequencing, developing, considering Murphy's Law, and building in the feedback mechanism.

Standards of nursing practice provide guidance in establishing frequency but may not be readily available. In the absence of written standards, establish consensus among team members. We'll discuss how to write procedures to insure standards of care in the next chapter. Another monitoring device is to schedule regular team conferences. If a goal is not being met, identify the reasons and revise the plan accordingly. If a goal is unrealistic, revise the goal. Make revisions right on the original care plan but do not obliterate revised items, since they provide valuable base data.

In addition, evaluating the client's progress is a critical part of the feedback mechanism. Progress notes should include reports on client progress, especially as related to expected outcomes, and thus complement the care plan. If the care plan is a part of the client's permanent record, then progress notes may be written on the plan in a separate evaluation column and separate notes eliminated.

Using this model helps make care planning less burdensome, since the activity is directed and purposeful. Approach care planning systematically and save time.

A Final Note on The Care Planning Process

Many professionals swear they have insufficient time to write care plans. Furthermore, they say, nobody uses care plans anyway because they're unrealistic. Both of these problems do exist but they are manageable. Manage time by writing and revising the care plan a piece at a time, in stages according to the client's priority problems. This way, the plan focuses on the client's greatest needs and develops as the situation does. Moreover, a plan which changes with the client tends to be realistic and therefore more useful. Writing an accurate, fully developed care plan for a client with multiple problems at one sitting, based only on initial assessment, is nigh unto impossible even when you have plenty of time. Do it in pieces based on the priority of client problems. A big job is only a set of small jobs.

The comprehensive care plan is a tool; use it dynamically to manage your client, your time, and your staff. Don't let it become a superficial operation and a burden.

Care Planning Guidelines

1. State client problems clearly.
2. Review and evaluate all available data.
3. Rank problems.
4. State goals clearly and specifically: include who, what, and when.
5. Rank goals.
6. Identify all actions necessary.
7. Use action verb format in the action plan.
8. Build in monitoring tools.
9. Begin care planning on admission.
10. Develop the plan piece by piece according to the priority of client needs.

Sample Care Plans

Mrs. H., 64, 195 lbs., 5′4″, was admitted last evening with cellulitis of her (R) foot and a 30 year history of diabetes mellitus. Five months ago she removed a callous from her foot with a razor blade. She did not notify her physician.

Her admission orders include:

NPH insulin 15 u. s.c. q̄ AM,
Gentamycin 8 mg q̄ 8 h IVMB,
Nafcillin Gm. ī q̄ 8 h IVMB,
Synthroid 0.1 mg q̄ AM (for 15 yr. of hypothyroidism),
Standard wound precautions,
Bedrest c̄ (R) leg ↑,
1500 cal ADA diet,
Betadine soaks q̄ shift to (R) foot,
Wet to Dry Betadine dressing to wound on (R) foot q̄ shift,
V/S q̄ 4 h.

During her dressing change @ 10 am she frowns and closes her eyes. The wound on her (R) foot is located over the first metatarsal joint. It is an open area 1/2″ deep, 1/2″ in diameter, and is draining yellowish, purulent material with a foul odor (amount difficult to determine as it blends with Betadine). Whitish-yellow tissue is visible throughout the wound. Her V/S at 10 AM are 100^{6}-96-24, B/P 150/94.

Several possible problems are present, including alteration in skin integrity related to cellulitis, knowledge deficit related to diabetic foot care, and knowledge deficit related to diabetic diet. Below are partial sample care plans. The plan for problem III is the dietitian's.

Sample Care Plan

DATE OF ADMISSION: 4/1/8-

CLIENT PROBLEM	EXPECTED OUTCOME	ACTION PLAN	EVALUATION
I. Impairment of skin integrity related to cellulitis (R) foot 4/1/8-.	I. A. Granulation tissue will be present throughout client's (R) foot ulcer by 4/8/8-.	I. A. 1. Provide bedrest with (R) leg elevated on two pillows. 2. Soak (R) foot in Betadine solution (250 cc. full-strength) × 20 minutes t.i.d. (10^A-4^P-10^P) 3. Dress (R) foot ulcer $\bar{p}$ each soak using W→D sterile techniques. a. Saturate 2 4×4's $\bar{c}$ Betadine Solution. b. Squeeze excess solution from each 4×4. c. Cover wound $\bar{c}$ the Betadine 4×4's. d. Place 2 dry 4×4's over Betadine gauzes. e. Wrap foot $\bar{c}$ 3″ Kling (not too tight).	I. A. 4/5/8- -No granulation tissue present. 4/8/8- -Minimal granulation tissue around outer edges of wound $\bar{c}$ eschar in center portion. Actions not effective in debriding wound. Try Elase treatments with saline gauze t.i.d. Re-evaluate in one week (4/15/8-). [Change plan in action column].
	B. (R) foot will not be swollen by 4/15/8-.	B. 1. Measure circumference of each foot. 2. Assess for degree of edema. 3. Elevate (R) leg on 2 pillows.	B. 4/15/8- -Both feet same circumference; no edema present.

Sample Care Plan, P 2

CLIENT PROBLEM	EXPECTED OUTCOME	ACTION PLAN	EVALUATION
II. Knowledge deficit related to diabetic foot care 4/1/8-.	II. A. Client will correctly state the rationale for proper foot care by 4/8/8-.	II. A. <u>Teach:</u> 1. Relationship of diabetes to decreased circulation. (Use p. 10 of standardized Diabetic Teaching Plan & flip chart.) 2. Definition & etiology of cellulitis. 3. Complications of poor foot care: cellulitis, gangrene, amputation.	II. A. 4/6/8- -Client stated that diabetics are prone to ASCVD due to plaque formation & circulation in feet; thus healing decreases. Action effective in improving knowledge $\overline{re}$ foot care.
	B. Client will demonstrate the preventive measures included in diabetic foot care by 4/15/8-.	B. <u>Teach:</u> 1. Importance of using mild soap (such as ivory) and H_2O for cleansing. 2. Importance of not "scrubbing" feet causing possible abrasion. 3. How to dry feet (especially between toes) by patting dry with soft towel. 4. How to inspect feet each day for abrasions or open areas. 5. Buerger-Allen exercises for increasing circulation.	B. 4/12/8- -Client only needed reinforcement of items 1-4 and 6-9. Client demonstrated the item 5 foot exercises.

Sample Care Plan, P 3

CLIENT PROBLEM	EXPECTED OUTCOME	ACTION PLAN	EVALUATION
		6. Not to cross legs. 7. Not to wear constrictive clothing, including girdles, garters, stockings, and shoes. 8. How to check pedal pulses. 9. Not to soak feet every day.	
	C. Client will describe the protocol for care of lesions on feet by 4/22/8-.	C. Teach: 1. Not to use iodine tincture solutions. 2. To keep open areas covered wth sterile bandage. 3. Not to cut callouses, corns, or toe nails. 4. To notify Dr. of any open or abrased areas on feet. 5. To go to podiatrist $\bar{q}$ 4-6 weeks for nail cutting.	C. 4/19/8- -Client did not recognize the importance of this aspect of her foot care. After teaching she stated that she realized her mistake of cutting her callous several weeks ago. 4/22/8- -Client described complete protocol as taught earlier in the week. Actions effective in increasing knowledge about diabetic foot care.

Sample Care Plan, P 4

CLIENT PROBLEM	EXPECTED OUTCOME	ACTION PLAN	EVALUATION
III. Knowledge deficit related to diabetic diet. 4/1/8-.	III. A. Client will develop a day's meal plan using diabetic exchange lists by 4/4/8-.	III. A. 1. Determine distribution of calorie allotment. 2. Explain design of each exchange list. 3. Explain how to interchange foods between lists. 4. Stress adherence to exact portions listed. 5. Demonstrate a sample meal. 6. Observe as client states a sample meal. 7. Provide feedback and reinforcement. 8. Observe as client states a day's meal plan. 9. Repeat steps A7 and A8 in two days and at discharge.	III. A. 4/4/8- -Client states calorie allocation and day's meal plan. 4/6/8- -Client states calorie allocation and day's meal plan without prompting.

Exercises

Exercise 1

Revise the sample statements of client problems below using the format prescribed by your agency.

Hemorrhage

____

____

Post-op complications

____

____

Teaching

____

____

Infection

____

____

Discharge planning

____

____

Pain

____

____

Premature ventricular contractions

____

____

Diabetes mellitus

____

____

Congenital hip dislocation

Immobility

Speech impairment

Hypertension

Exercise 2

Prepare a sample goal/intended outcome statement for each of the above problems.

Exercise 3

Revise the action statements below, making them clearer and more specific.

Encourage ambulation

Provide emotional support

Push fluids

Do diabetic teaching

Monitor hemorrhage

Avoid stress

Provide a quiet environment

Exercise 4

Review the following cases. Follow the instructions provided.

Case 1

Mrs. W., 27, was admitted two days ago for an emergency cholecystectomy. Today you are assigned to care for her during the 7-3 shift. Her orders are:

IV D5/1/2 NS @ 125 cc hr,
Keflin Gm ī q̄ 4 h IVMB,
Demerol 75 mg c̄ Vistaril 25 mg IM q̄ prn pain,
NPO,
V/S q̄ 4 h,
Incentive spirometer q̄ 2 h,
DB + C q̄ h,
I + O.

When checking her dressing, you note that her abdomen is taut and distended; bowel sounds are absent. She reports generalized abdominal discomfort, particularly on light palpation. Her abdominal dressing is dry and intact. Vitals are 101°-100-22, B/P 130/78 @ 10 am.

She has a productive cough with copious amounts of whitish, foamy sputum. You report your findings to the physician, after giving her prn pain medication.

Identify one client problem. Write a care plan using the following format. (Evaluation, of course, would only occur after the plan is in effect.) See Table 3-1 for nursing diagnoses developed to date.

Case 2

Mrs. H., 64, 195 lbs., 5′4″, had a below the knee right leg amputation one week ago. Her doctor has ordered physical therapy.

Identify one client problem. Write a care plan using the following format. (Evaluation, of course, would only occur after the plan is in effect.) See Table 3-1 for nursing diagnoses developed to date.

CLIENT PROBLEM	EXPECTED OUTCOME	ACTION PLAN	EVALUATION

Chapter 4
Writing Procedures

Objectives

After reading this chapter and completing the exercises, you should be able to write procedures.

Specifically, in this chapter, you learn to:

- Identify the elements in developing procedures.
- Apply the elements of this process.
- Evaluate sample procedures.
- Revise and correct faulty procedures.

A ***procedure*** or ***protocol*** is simply a how-to explanation which enables the reader to carry out a particular task in the simplest, most efficient, most accurate way. Every health care agency publishes a manual of important procedures and makes copies available to staff. Indeed, you can expect to be asked to contribute to the manual. The test of the procedure writer's effectiveness is the result the reader produces. The writer can assume nothing and must provide explicit step by step directions.

Follow this process to develop clear procedures:

1. State the task to be performed.
2. State the purpose.
3. Identify tools, supplies, equipment.
4. List all the steps necessary to complete the task by:
   a. observing,
   b. performing,
   c. simulating, or
   d. brainstorming the task.
5. State steps in performance terms.
6. Break the steps into the smallest possible pieces. List substeps.
7. Place the steps in the most efficient sequence.
8. Consider Murphy's Law. Build in preventive and protective actions.
9. Check for:
   a. accuracy,
   b. completeness,
   c. clarity, and
   d. practicality.

State the Task

Name the task to be performed as specifically as possible, so that users can differentiate easily among similar tasks. For example, a task which involves assisting with a procedure should be clearly titled.

Example:

Assisting with Surgical Dressing Change

State the Purpose

An effective complement to naming the task clearly is to add a purpose statement which briefly explains the reasons for performing the task. Display this statement immediately below the title.

Example:

Taking the Blood Pressure

Purpose:

To aid in assessment.
To monitor changes in client conditions.

In basic procedures, such as taking vital signs, the purpose is self evident; in more complex procedures, however, spell out the purpose for the audience. A reader who understands the intended outcome of the task is more likely to carry out the task properly than is one who does not.

Identify Tools, Supplies, Equipment

Next, list all implements and materials necessary to perform the task. Display this list below the purpose statement. While drafting the procedure, don't worry if you forget some item; as you develop the steps in the process, you'll recall anything that eludes you here.

Example:

Gather the following equipment:

A. Stethoscope
B. Sphygmomanometer
C. Alcohol Swab

APPLICATION:
Select a simple task which you perform frequently. State the the task and its purpose clearly. Then list any tools or equipment needed.

Task:

____

____

Purpose:

____

____

Supplies:

____

____

____

____

List all Steps Necessary to Complete the Task

The most efficient way to perform this step, if you are doing a motor task, is to find someone who is expert in the task and observe that person's performance while you take notes and ask questions. Capture all the steps that way, and in order.

If this approach is impossible, perform the task yourself; if you know how, list steps as you go along. If the tools, supplies, or equipment to do the task are unavailable, simulate the task.

Use the observation method whenever possible, since using this method allows you to concentrate on writing, not doing the task. Moreover, observation assumes that you are not an expert in performing the task. Performance and simulation require expertise and also that you do two things at once, perform and analyze. Whenever you are unfamiliar with the task, validate your analysis with someone who is competent in the task.

Brainstorming is perhaps the best method of listing steps when the task you are analyzing is a managerial, interpersonal, or similar task which is difficult to recreate physically. For example, you wish to develop a procedure for managing clients who resist following directions. Often the best way to do so is to meet with those individuals who most frequently deal with these clients and develop a list of actions cooperatively.

Don't worry, at this point, whether the steps are in order or not. Here the major concern is identifying all of them; later you will put them in sequence.

State Steps in *Performance Terms*

As you list steps, regardless of the method you use, state them in action verb phrases. These performance terms clarify the intent of each step and make the procedure easy to follow. Each step is a command.

Example:

Rather than simply listing equipment, say "Gather the following equipment and supplies," listing the items needed next.

Rather than "client should be resting in a comfortable position," say "Place client in a comfortable position."

Each item in the procedure is grammatically a command: ***Place, Raise, Lift, Remove, Record.*** Each is a complete thought followed by a period. The directions for writing procedures illustrate this action verb format.

If a statement requires qualifiers, place them after the action verb statement. For example, phrases specifying ***if*** and ***when*** should follow the action: "Allow pressure to fall to zero, ***if*** second reading is needed."

APPLICATION:

Analyze the task you chose in the last Application box. List the steps needed to carry out the task. State each step in performance terms.

Steps to carry out for selected task:

____

____

____

____

____

____

____

____

Break into Smallest Pieces

Review the steps and ask if each is clear, discrete, and self contained. When any step requires more than one discrete action, subdivide it.

Remember that the audience you are trying to reach doesn't know how to do this task—that's why you're writing the procedure. The smaller the parts of the tasks, the more readily the person learning can grasp your instructions. On the other hand, if the step requires two closely related actions which constitute parts of the same flow, leave the two actions together.

Example:

Take and record vital signs.
Open victim's mouth and check for contents.

Once you've identified substeps, list them beneath the major step they subdivide. State substeps, of course, in action verb format. Note the substeps for this process at the beginning of the chapter.

Place in Sequence

Next you are ready to place the steps in the most efficient sequence. If you have used the observation method, they may already be, but don't assume. Review the list, being particularly careful that steps that rely on the completion of previous steps follow those steps: a reliance dependency is a relationship in which one action cannot occur until another is completed. For example, you must mount a bicycle before you can pedal it; you must locate a vein before you can inject it. In sequencing, consider reliance dependencies, the client's comfort and safety, and the logic of the task itself. Client comfort dictates that you check the location and tightness of the blood pressure cuff before inflating it. The logic of the task suggests that you gather tools, supplies, and equipment before commencing the task since you don't want to complete part of the task, then stop, and scurry off to find a pair of forceps.

If you're not sure what the best sequence is, try the task several ways and select the order which yields the best results. Again, don't assume: in particular, don't assume that the way a task has always been done is necessarily the best way.

Number the steps; use letters to label substeps, unless only one occurs; then just highlight it with a dash. This format is readily comprehensible to the reader and quite easy to follow.

APPLICATION:
Continue with the task you selected above. Below, organize the steps you listed in what you believe to be the most efficient order.
The best sequence is:

1. ______________________________
2. ______________________________
3. ______________________________
4. ______________________________
5. ______________________________
6. ______________________________
7. ______________________________
8. ______________________________

Consider Murphy's Law

> "Whatever can go wrong, will go wrong, and at the worst possible time."
> —Murphy

Ask yourself, at this point, "What can go wrong?" Where pitfalls are possible, build into the step preventive or protective action. Preventive action forestalls "whatever can go wrong" from going wrong. If a pitfall is impossible to prevent, build in action that will minimize the negative impact of whatever can go wrong.

> "Nothing is as easy as it looks."
> —Murphy

Review each step carefully for potential disaster. Building in preventive or protective action could save a client's life and will certainly save time. Consider using an illustration to clarify any step which might be misunderstood.

Example:

In describing the process for taking a rectal temperature, be sure to direct the temperature taker to hold on to the thermometer, once inserted, to prevent breakage or loss into the lower bowel. The procedure for taking the pulse should include the directive to see that the artery isn't constricted, since constriction will make the pulse difficult or impossible to feel.

Protective action would include measures such as sponge bathing in a water/alcohol mixture if the client's temperature reaches a certain level, or notifying the charge nurse of certain changes in the client's condition.

"Left to themselves, all things go
from bad to worse."
—Murphy.

Don't think that you can avoid pitfalls by ignoring them. They won't go away. Invest the time now to build your procedures properly and you will collect dividends later.

Check

Finally, review your procedure, step by step, for accuracy, completeness, clarity, and practicality. Be sure that each step states exactly what the practitioner must do, and eliminate any step that's redundant. Apply the procedure, at least by simulation, and be sure that all the steps are there, and in the proper order. Check for consistent use of action verb format so that each step is clear, and while simulating, verify that each step is done most easily as you've described it.

Now you have a completed procedure. Don't just write it up and forget it. Review each procedure yearly and revise and update as needed as a result of changes in hospital policy, equipment, and state of the art practice, or in response to your own experience.

APPLICATION:
Using the procedure you've developed so far, check each step for pitfalls. If you find any, list them below. Then, double check your procedure for action verb format, efficient sequence, and completeness. Be sure each step is as small as possible.

	Step	Pitfalls
1.	______________________	______________________
2.	______________________	______________________
3.	______________________	______________________
4.	______________________	______________________
5.	______________________	______________________
6.	______________________	______________________
7.	______________________	______________________
8.	______________________	______________________

Sample Procedure

Now let's look at a sample procedure. The various elements we've discussed are labelled to illustrate the process described:

TAKING THE BLOOD PRESSURE

A. Purpose:
   1. To aid in diagnosis.
   2. To monitor changes in client condition.

B. Procedure:
   1. Gather the following equipment:
      a. sphygmomanometer.
      b. stethoscope.
      c. alcohol swab.
   2. Check chart for range of blood pressure readings.
   3. Explain procedure to client.

4. Quiet room; Remove visitors.
5. Place client in relaxed, comfortable position, sitting unless otherwise specified by physician. Allow client to recover from any recent exercise or excitement; exercise or excitement may increase systolic pressure.
6. Expose the left arm to the shoulder or the left leg to the groin.
   a. Roll clothing well above the joint.
   b. Eliminate constrictions of the extremities.
7. Wrap completely deflated cuff about limb snugly and smoothly.
   a. Place rubber bladder over brachial artery in arm or lower popliteal artery in leg.
   b. Place lower edge of cuff one inch above joint.
   c. Avoid limb which is paralyzed, has an IV site or shunt, or from which blood has been recently drawn.
   d. Avoid side of recent mastectomy.
   e. Be sure cuff is comfortable; fit correct size to client.
8. Palpate the brachial artery at the inner side of the bend of the elbow or popliteal artery in the popliteal space behind the knee.
9. Place stethoscope over point of strongest pulse.
   a. Avoid stethoscope contact with cuff.
   b. Hold diaphragm gently but fully in contact with client's skin. Reading will be altered by overly tight pressure.
10. Close valve of cuff by tightening screw near air bulb to prevent air from escaping cuff.
11. Inflate cuff until pulse is obliterated in limb.
12. Release air from cuff slowly by loosening screw near bulb. Read gauge on first beat heard; this is systolic pressure.

13. Continue cuff deflation. Read gauge on last beat heard; this is diastolic pressure.
    a. Record the points at which muffled or dulled sounds occur, or under hemodynamic conditions, no cessation of sounds occurs.
    b. Allow pressure to fall to zero if second reading is needed.
14. Remove cuff. Cleanse stethoscope and diaphragm earpieces with alcohol swab to prevent cross-contamination.
15. Record on vital sign worksheet: time; readings; position, when so ordered; limb used, if applicable.

Note that the procedure above is in a readable outline format, that each item is an action verb statement, and that each step is numbered. Accessible to the reader, this format is easy to understand.

Procedure Writing Guidelines

1. Name the task and purpose clearly.
2. Identify all tools, supplies, materials.
3. List all steps.
4. Use action verbs.
5. Divide steps into their smallest pieces.
6. Organize the steps efficiently.
7. Remember Murphy's Law.
8. Double check the finished product.
9. Number all steps. Use letters for substeps.
10. Use outline form.

Exercises

Exercise 1

Review the following procedures. Revise as needed to conform to the format presented in this chapter.

PROCEDURE FOR TEMPERATURE TAKING

I. Purpose:
To monitor any physiological changes in the body both prophylactically and in the presence of an on-going disease process.

II. Equipment:	Key Points:
1. Glass thermometer and holder	1. Blue-oral; red-rectal
2. Alcohol swabs	
3. Lubricant	3. For rectal temperature method

III. Procedure:

A. Oral Method	
1. Check to see that the mercury has been shaken down before use.	
2. Place thermometer under the client's tongue for three minutes.	2. Client should be alert, oriented, and not a mouth breather.
3. Read the thermometer, clean with an alcohol swab, shake down mercury and then replace in dry container.	

B. Rectal Method	
1. Check to see that the mercury has been shaken down before use.	1. Use rectal technique for unconscious clients, clients with oxygen, and others for whom oral method is not advised.

2. Place lubricated tip of thermometer in the rectum about 1-1/2″ and hold in position for 5 minutes.

   2. Holding the thermometer will prevent breakage or loss into the lower bowel.

C. Axillary Method

1. Check to see that the mercury has been shaken down before use.
2. Place thermometer in axilla, tip upward and cross arm over chest securing it in place. Leave in place 10 to 15 minutes.

   2. Use axillary method when rectal is contra-indicated and oral method is not feasible.

3. Read the thermometer, clean with a alcohol swab, shake down mercury and replace in dry container.

IV. Charting:

1. Report any unusually high or low temperatures to the doctor immediately.

   1. Remember that temperature may vary with physical and emotional changes, with clothing, and with food intake.

2. Record temperature on vital sign sheet under specified time. Frequency is determined by the physician's order.
3. Chart any unusual observation of the client. (i.e., painful hemorrhoid, no teeth, etc.)

TAKING THE PULSE

A. Purpose:	Key Points
To determine the client's condition by means of the heart beat.	

B. General Instructions:

	Key Points
1. The pulse may be counted in arteries lying near the surface of the body which may be compressed against an underlying bone. a. The radial—wrist b. The facial—edge of lower jaw c. The carotid—on each side of throat d. The temporal—in front of external ear e. The femoral—groin f. The dorsalis pedal—foot g. Posterial tibal—medial aspect ankle h. popliteal—post. aspect knee	
2. Do not use too much pressure.	2. Pulse may be obliterated.
3. Do not use thumb to feel pulse.	3. Pulsation of artery in one's thumb may be mistaken for client's pulse.
4. Client should be quiet at rest when pulse is taken.	4. Pulse is affected by exercise, eating, stimulants, emotions, depressants and extremes of heat and cold.
5. Be sure that the artery is not constricted.	
6. Points to be observed: 1. Rate 2. Tension 3. Rhythm 4. Volume	

C. Equipment:
   1. Watch with second hand

D. Procedure:
   1. Place two or three fingers over the artery with light pressure.
   2. Count the number of beats for 15 seconds and multiply by four; or for 30 seconds and multiply by two; or for full minute if pulse is irregular.
   3. Observe the general character of the pulse.

E. Charting:
   1. On vital sign work sheet under appropriate time.

      1. This is graphed on the vital signs sheet in the client's chart usually by the unit secretary.

   2. On Nursing Observation Notes, make note of any abnormalities in volume rate or regularity.
   3. Special Chart—When pulse is taken more frequently than q4h, it should be recorded on the special chart.
   4. Signature (first initial, last name, classification) on nursing observation notes and special chart.

SURGICAL DRESSING CHANGE

I. Purpose:
To change surgical dressing for purpose of:
— preventing infection;
— observing and cleansing wounds;
— preventing irritation of the skin; and
— preventing odor.

II. General Instructions:
1. The doctor will do the first dressing change post operatively.
2. The doctor will write order for dressing to be changed (as necessary, q.d.).
3. A dressing may be reinforced as necessary.
4. An order will be written if a cleansing agent, ointment, or medication is to be applied to the skin.
5. A wound culture is done if indicated.

III. Equipment:
The amount and type of equipment to be used will depend on the location and size of area to be dressed.
The following supplies are commonly needed:
1. Sterile 4x4's (2x2s if needed)
2. Sterile abdominal pads (ABD's)
3. Sterile gloves
4. Sterile barrier
5. Sterile Kelly and/or forceps
6. Paper bag to receive soiled dressing (waxed bag)
7. Montgomery straps (if needed)
8. Tape
9. Cleansing agent (as prescribed), Betadine swabs are often used

IV. Procedure:	Key Points:
1. Obtain supplies as needed and check treatment kardex for specific order.	1. Supplies from S.P.D. cart in clean holding area.
2. Explain procedure to client.	
3. Position client and expose area to be dressed.	
4. Place waxed paper bag in a convenient place.	4. Obtain from central supply. To receive soiled dressing.

5. Open sterile barrier on a clean dry surface. Open and place needed 4x4s, ABD pads, forceps, on sterile barrier.	
6. Remove the soiled dressing using forceps and place in waxed paper bag.	6. Note amount of drainage and condition of area. Forceps are now contaminated and must not be placed back on sterile field.
7. Open Betadine swabs.	
8. Using sterile gloved hand and forcep or clamp, clean area.	8. Clean area gently with cleansing solution or Betadine swabs. Clean area around wound working from center of area outward in a circular motion.
9. Replace dressings:	
a. Place 4x4s around and over wound using sterile technique.	
b. Place sterile ABD pads on top of dressing and fasten with tape or PRN (montgomery) straps.	b. Apply binder if ordered. Change PRN straps as necessary.
10. Care of Equipment:	
a. Bag with soiled dressing and barrier to be be placed in soiled holding room in large waxed refuse bag.	a. Ring stand with large refuse bag in soiled holding.
b. Instruments to be washed and placed in soiled holding room.	b. To S.P.D. for resterilization.

V. Charting:

1. Record on Nursing Observation Notes:
   Pertinent information concerning condition of skin, drainage (if any) amount and type.
2. Chart if culture is done.
3. Signature of nurse.

Exercise 2

Prepare a procedure explaining one of the following tasks. Use the format presented.

a. Teaching a staff member how to use an infusion pump (or some other simple device).
b. Teaching a client how to tie shoes.
c. Conducting an employment interview or employee evaluation interview.
d. Teaching a client to brush teeth.

Exercise 3

Select a simple task with which you are familiar. Simulate or perform the task and prepare a procedure using the format presented.

Exercise 4

Observe a colleague performing a task with which you are unfamiliar. Prepare a procedure using the format presented.

Unit II
Writing in the Professional Setting

Introduction

Many of you have some special skill or knowledge to offer, an idea or insight to share, or method or approach to demonstrate. Perhaps you seek to apply a unique ability in a job; perhaps you wish to explain a new insight in an article. Unit II of The Writer's Handbook helps you communicate that different concept or talent to its intended audience.

Chapter 5, "Selling Your Professional Self," presents techniques for preparing an effective resumé or vita and discusses the differences between the two. The chapter also includes direction in writing a letter of introduction that will help get your vita or resumé noticed and get you interviewed. By the end of the chapter, you'll have constructed a vita, resumé, and letter.

Chapter 6, "Writing for Publication," explores the "ins" and "outs" of identifying a market, focusing on an audience, writing a query letter, planning and executing the potential article, working revisions, and other aspects of the process of getting published. By the end of the chapter, you'll have organized a sample article and query.

Chapter 7, "Writing Memoranda and Letters," completes Unit II of this text. The focus here is on clear, straightforward communication which simplifies internal and external messages. By the end of the chapter, you'll have sample memoranda and letters which will help you commmunicate more effectively.

In order to supply concrete illustrations of the kinds of product in question, we've again offered samples to use as models or to critique. Each chapter proceeds in step by step fashion, so that you can master each component of the process readily and then manage the whole. Exercises throughout help you to apply the skills you've learned.

Chapter 5
Selling Your Professional Self

Objectives

After reading this chapter and completing the exercises, you will be able to prepare a curriculum vita, a resumé, and a letter of introduction.

Specifically in this chapter you learn to:

Identify and apply the elements of planning and organizing:

- a curriculum vita.
- a resumé.
- a letter of introduction.

Communicating effectively with someone whose approval you need—whether to get a job or to get admitted to an educational program—is critical. Your ability to sell your credentials is as important as the credentials themselves. Your sales kit is your curriculum vita (CV), resumé, and letter of introduction. Preparing these tools in a planned, systematic way makes the job easier and the product more effective. This chapter suggests a process for developing and renewing these sales tools which will help you direct attention to your strengths and thus display your wares attractively.

Writing Your Curriculum Vita (CV)

The CV is a formal, comprehensive document, which displays your skills, abilities, and experience. Include all your significant academic, work related, and personal experiences.

The process of developing a CV is relatively simple:

1. List all potentially useful information.
2. Categorize the information.
3. Organize the information chronologically within categories.
4. Rank the categories.
5. Develop fully but concisely.
6. Prepare an overview.
7. Design an accessible, consistent format.
8. Proofread carefully.

List all potentially useful information. Start now and move backward or start at birth and move forward, but whatever you do, proceed logically. In other words, pick a logical starting point and brainstorm, using time to help you organize your recollections. List everything you've done which might be useful to a potential employer or educational program. At this point, don't be selective. Date each item by month and year as you proceed. Don't worry about listing items in exact order; concentrate on recalling as much as possible. Recalling certain events will trigger recalling others, but often in scrambled order.

Check your files for certificates, diplomas, awards, letters of commendation, and the like. Call former teachers, classmates, employers, or fellow workers to help you reconstruct dates or events, if necessary. If your memory is cloudy, construct a timeline and try to remember anything that occurred during a given period to stimulate recall. For example, here's a timeline for 1978:

January	CPR
February	first aid course
March	
April	
May	Graduated from college
June	Worked at camp
July	
August	Part-time job at clinic
September	
October	Took state boards
November	
December	

Fill in whatever you can recall and go from there. When you finish this first step of the CV process, you'll have a shopping list of potentially useful items.

Categorize the information. Now you're ready to organize your list. Select categories based on the nature of the items listed. Likely categories are education, work experience, and personal background. Important items which might not fit these categories could be classified "other" or used to generate an additional category. Label each item on your list by category, like this:

1978, January:	CPR-education
February:	First aid course-education
May:	Graduated college-education
June:	Worked at camp-work
August:	Part-time job at clinic-work

When you've completed this step, you'll have a list of items classified by category.

APPLICATION:

Construct a timeline and list information which is potentially useful in CV preparation. Categorize and label the information as E = Education, W = Work experience, P = Personal background, O = Other. You are constructing a draft CV.

E(Education)	W(Work experience)	P(Personal)	O(Other)

Organize chronologically. Now you're ready to rewrite your list in chronological order, dividing it into categories as you go. Select any category and list items in that category beginning with the most recent and working backwards, including month and year. As you list, expand items as necessary to make them clear and specific. Your revised list will look something like this:

Education	
May, 1978:	BSW, University of Maryland, with honors.
February, 1978:	First aid course, American Red Cross.
January, 1978:	CPR certificate, American Heart Association.

Complete this process for each category. Now you have an organized set of data, some of which will appear in your CV. Save this list and update it periodically. If you keep your overall list on file and keep it current, then you can customize a CV for any type of situation. Select items to place in the customized CV based on your intended audience, when possible. Tell your audience what you know or have done which prepares you for success in a given setting. For example, if you are applying for a specialized educational program such as basic critical care, using a particular clinical machine, or crisis intervention, select items accordingly.

You can also prepare a general CV which includes multiple categories of numerous items for use in situations where the intended audience is unclear or where you know that the audience is looking for a well rounded individual. An example of such a situation would be applying for an entry level position.

Rank categories. The general practice is to order the categories as follows: education, work experience, personal background, other. Vary this order when you believe that your audience values one category above the others. For example, if you are seeking a supervisory job, work experience might be more important to your audience than the other categories. The order above, however, is suitable for most situations.

Create additional categories when you find clusters of like items in "other." For example, additional categories might include professional organizations, community activities, awards and honors, publications, offices held, or a variety of other classifications. Place these categories in priority relation with your other categories based on your audience. If you apply for the position of vice president of your professional organization, then, place the "professional organizations and offices held" categories at or near the top.

APPLICATION:

Rank the categories in your draft CV.

E(Education)	W(Work experience)	P(Personal)	O(Other)

Develop fully but concisely. Next you must explain each item you've selected for your CV. Be sure to eliminate those which shed no light on your ability to perform in the type of situation for which you are applying.

Expand each item using a standard formula. For education, state the institution attended, the degree earned, and major field of study, where the degree designation isn't specific. For continuing education or inservice courses, state the course taken and the sponsoring agency. Refer to the sample in this chapter for examples. For work experience, state the job title; whether the job was full or part-time; the place of employment; the major duties, tasks, and responsibilities; and the reason for leaving, if needed. Don't include the salary earned. That will appear on the employment application.

Example:

August, 1978:	Nursing assistant, 20 hours per week, River Pediatric Hospital, Kazoo, Michigan. Prepared clients for physical examination. Took and recorded vital signs. Assisted physician with therapeutic procedures. Transported clients. Completed lab and x-ray forms. Left to seek full time employment as social worker.

For personal background, present your birth date, health status, and such additional information as marital and parental status, height and weight, and personal interests and hobbies. Use your judgment here as to how much you wish to present; birth date and health status are standard items on many CV's, but the other items are optional.

Present sufficient detail so that your audience gets a clear picture of your accomplishments and background. Use as few words as possible, however, to make your point. In the work experience example above, action verb phrases—"prepared clients. . .," "transported clients. . ."—state duties concisely. After developing each item, read it over and eliminate any unnecessary words.

For additional categories, decide in advance what formula to use for developing items. Stick to your formula to assure consistency.

APPLICATION: Develop each item in your draft CV fully.

Prepare an overview. Now that you've developed and organized the CV, you're ready to write a brief summary which will serve as an introduction. This overview gives the reader a condensed glimpse of your qualifications, and provides an effective spot to display your professional goals. Select three or four essential items from the body of the CV and present them in one or two terse sentences; close with a goal statement. Write the overview after you've done the rest of the CV; that way you'll have a clear idea of which key elements to include. See our sample CV for an example.

APPLICATION: Write your overview.

Design an accessible, consistent format. Type your CV. Start by centering your full name at the top of the page. Place your home address and phone number on the left side of the page, about 10 spaces in. Next, place your business address and phone number on the right side of the page parallel to the home address and number. The information should look balanced and symmetrical. Any other format which presents the same material attractively is acceptable as an alternative to this suggestion.

Next present each category in its priority order. Label each category clearly; center and underline each label. Present each label in the same form—begin each word with capitals, for example. Within categories, list dates, month, then year, starting with the most recent. Then follow the formula you've developed for that category.

As you present each category, check for completeness. Eliminate major time gaps and try to remember any important activities or experiences not listed.

Organize each category so that it looks like all the others. Use the same spacing, margins, indentations, capitalization, and punctuation throughout. Avoid abbreviations; acronyms, like RN, RT, PT, and ADA are usually acceptable, however.

Proofread carefully. All of your efforts are undone if the finished product is marred by grammatical or typographical errors. Such flaws often repulse prospective employers or admissions personnel.

Double check spellings and punctuations of which you are unsure. If corrections are impossible, retype the document. Have a fresh reader, friend, or colleague review the product before sending it out. Often such a reader can spot problems you miss due to your familiarity with the material.

Sample Curriculum Vita

Diana D. Irving

Home Address:	**Business Address:**
0000 Moravia Avenue	University of Maryland
Baltimore, Maryland 00000	School of Nursing
(301) 555-0000	655 West Lombard Street
	Baltimore, Maryland 00000
	(301) 555-0000

Professional Goal

Thoroughly grounded in instruction and program development and coordination, I seek a position which will allow me to apply my professional experience as well as my advanced academic credentials. Such a position would include both teaching and management opportunities.

Education

Fall, 198-	Began part-time study in Ph.D. in nursing program at University of Maryland, Baltimore, Maryland..
May, 198-	Master of Science, with Nursing Education as role, Medical-Surgical Nursing as area of concentration, Rheumatology Nursing as clinical specialty, University of Maryland, Baltimore, Maryland.
May, 197-	Bachelor of Science in Nursing, University of Maryland, Baltimore, Maryland.
August, 196-	Diploma, Peninsula General Hospital School of Nursing, Salisbury, Maryland.
June, 196-	Diploma, J. M. Bennett Senior High School, Salisbury, Maryland.

Work Experience

February, 198- Present	Nursing Instructor, University of Maryland School of Nursing, Baltimore, Maryland; Taught Junior Year Concepts I and II courses, includes classroom and clinical instruction in medical surgical nursing; Member of Curriculum Revision Committee; Taught Legislative Elective.
197-198-	Nursing Instructor, Union Memorial School of Nursing. Taught Medical-Surgical Nursing II, and Medical-Surgical Nursing IB course in Summer, 198-; Presented extensive classroom and clinical instruction in both courses; During 198--198- served as Second Level Chairman; Member, Curriculum Committee; Member, Library Committee; Member, Faculty Organization and Junior Class Advisor. On leave, 198--198-.
198--198-	Nursing Instructor, Staff Development, Good Samaritan Hospital, Baltimore, Maryland; Presented classes in rheumatology nursing, medical-surgical nursing, and documentation for nursing staff at all levels; Taught in the first nursing internship program.
197-	Nursing Instructor, Community College of Baltimore, Baltimore, Maryland; Taught in medical-surgical nursing course for third semester students.
197--197-	Nursing Instructor, DHMH School of Practical Nursing, Baltimore, Maryland; Presented classroom and clinical content in medical-surgical and obstetric nursing.
197--197-	Nurse Training Specialist, Staff Development, University of Maryland Hospital, Baltimore, Maryland; Oriented new nurses, developed nursing assistant course, gave classes to all levels of nursing staff on all shifts; Kept clinically current by working as staff member on neurosurgical unit.
197--197-.	Health/Nutrition Coordinator, Project Head Start, Salisbury, Maryland; Managed health and health education for 225 preschool children in two counties, the teaching staff, dietary staff, and the families of the Head Start children; Supervised health and dietary staff.

196--197-.	Staff Nurse/Charge Nurse, Peninsula General Hospital, Salisbury, Maryland; Provided care for medical-surgical patients.

Professional Organizations

National/Maryland League for Nursing, member, President (198--198-); Served on Meet the Authors Committee, 198--present; 198- Convention Committee; as Co-Chairman, 198- Convention Committee; and as Chairperson, Public Affairs Committee, 198-.

Sigma Theta Tau; inducted in 197-.

National Arthritis Foundation, AHP Section, 198--present; Maryland AHP Section, Education Committee Chairman; Program Committee member, 198--198-, Southeastern AHPA, Ad Hoc Committee on Long-Range Planning for Maryland AHP Section, 198-.

American Nurses' Association; member, Maryland Legislative Committee, 198--present.

Maryland Association of Health Science Educators; Secretary, 198--198-; Member of Board of Directors, 197--198-.

Maryland Society for Rheumatic Diseases, 198--198-.

Awards and Honors

198-	Award for excellence in Nursing Education University of Maryland (departmental award for graduating graduate student).
197-	Sigma Theta Tau.
	High Honors for B.S.N.
	Phi Kappa Phi candidate.
196--196-	Senatorial, Board of Trustees, and Moose Organization scholarships for basic nursing education.
196-	National Honor Society induction.
196--196-	Academic Achievement Awards, 10th, 11th, 12th grades.

Creative Works

Master's Thesis

Irving, Diana D. "Technical Competence of Registered Nurses in the Administration of Oral Medications." (University of Maryland, 198-).

Publications

Irving, Diana. "Clinical Competence of New Graduates: A Study to Measure Performance." The Journal of Continuing Education in Nursing (July/August, 198-).

Irving, Diana and Lord, Phyllis. "The Technical Competence of Registered Nurses in the Administration of Oral Medications." The Journal of Nursing Education (198-).

Irving, Diana and Gregory, John. "Job Analysis: The Basis of Effective Appraisal." The Journal of Nursing Administration (July/August, 198-).

Irving, Diana and Gregory, John. "Charting: Simplify the Task." RN Magazine (March, 198-).

Other Work-Related Activities

198--present Faculty Consultant in Rheumatology and Orthopedic Nursing for Resource Applications, Inc., Baltimore, Maryland.

198--198- Instructor for continuing education programs for nurses in rheumatology at Howard Community College, Health and Education Council.

Community Service Activities

198--198- Arthritis Foundation, Speakers' Bureau member, and Public Education Committee member.

197--198- Member and committee member, Walker Community Association.

197--197- Member, Lupus Foundation; chair, staff development on group process.

Hobbies

Bowling, sewing, gardening, reading.

Special Interests

Rheumatology Nursing.
Research in Nursing Education.
Evaluation in Nursing Education.
Chronic and Long-Term Care.

Personal Information

Born: December 20, 194-.
Married, one child, born 196-.
Height: 5′6″.
Weight: 130 pounds.
Health: Excellent.

References

On request.

Preparing the Resumé

The major difference between the CV and the resumé is depth of development. The resumé is essentially an abstract of the CV; thus the process of developing the resumé is quite similar. Obviously, one way to proceed is simply to condense the CV, customizing it for your intended audience. When possible, contact the party to whom you are applying. Inquire about the institution's or organization's needs and expectations, and develop your resumé accordingly.

No firm consensus exists on the "best" length or the "best" format for a resumé. Generally, however, certain guidelines are useful:

1. Be brief; 2-3 pages maximum, double spaced.
2. Present attractively; use categories to organize and white space to highlight.
3. Create focus; emphasize your most important assets and experiences.
4. Customize; create the focus to meet the needs of your particular audience.

If you have not done a CV, refer to the process explained in the first section of this chapter and:

1. List potentially useful information for your audience.
2. Categorize.
3. Organize chronologically.
4. Prioritize.
5. Eliminate the least important items.
6. Develop remaining items very briefly.
7. Prepare a highly condensed overview directed to your audience.
8. Design an accessible format.
9. Proofread carefully.

If you have one, work from your CV to:

1. Select the most important items which relate to your audience.
2. Condense the items.
3. Retain the categories which remain, revising as needed.
4. Condense the overview, with a modified focus, if needed.
5. Present accessibly.

Select the most important/eliminate the least important items. Cut your list of items or CV from the bottom up. Use only items which are absolutely indispensible to your audience. Delete the rest. Remember, you are working with 2 to 3 pages at most.

Condense/develop briefly. Put some flesh on the skeleton of each item, but include only the most critical and relevant duties or accomplishments. Restrict yourself to about two lines per item.

Categorize/revise categories. Group similar items in categories customized to your audience. In our sample resumé, "Related Professional Experience" zeroes in on experience indirectly related to teaching, but shows clinical and practical experience. "Current Professional Organizations" and "Recent Publications" limit the time frame presented and feature items which are complementary to teaching.

Condense the overview. Write directly to the audience; highlight one or two key points which emphasize your unique qualifications or accomplishments.

Present accessibly. Outline your material so that white space, capital letters, and underscoring highlight each important item, as in the sample that follows.

This sample resumé is based on the sample CV in this chapter. It's customized for a teaching position in an undergraduate nursing program.

Sample Resumé

Diana D. Irving
0000 Moravia Avenue
Baltimore, Maryland 00000
(301) 555-0000

Professional Goal

Experienced in instruction and program coordination, I seek a teaching position which challenges both my instructional skills and my academic background.

Education

Fall, 198-	Began part-time Ph.D. program in nursing at University of Maryland.
May 198-	***Master of Science,*** Nursing Education, University of Maryland.
May, 197-	***Bachelor of Science in Nursing,*** University of Maryland.
August, 196-	***Diploma,*** Peninsula General Hospital School of Nursing.

Related Teaching Experience

February, 198- –present	***Nursing Instructor, University of Maryland School*** *of Nursing*. Duties include clinical instruction as well as curriculum development.
197--198-	***Nursing Instructor, Union Memorial School of Nursing.*** Taught Medical-Surgical nursing; served on curriculum committee. On leave 198--8-.
198--198-	***Nursing Instructor, Good Samaritan Hospital.*** Presented in-service programs in rheumatology and medical-surgical nursing and in documentation.
197-	***Nursing Instructor, Community College of Baltimore.*** Taught medical surgical nursing.
197--197-	***Nursing Instructor, DHMH School of Practical Nursing.*** Taught medical-surgical and obstetric nursing.

Related Professional Experience

197--197-	***Health/Nutrition Coordinator, Project Head Start.*** Managed health and health education programs for clients; supervised staff.
196--197-	***Staff Nurse/Charge Nurse, Peninsula General Hospital.*** Worked on Medical-Surgical unit.

Current Professional Organizations

National/Maryland League for Nursing; President, 198--198-.
Sigma Theta Tau; inducted 197-.
Maryland Association of Health Science Educators; Secretary 198--198-; Board of Directors, 197--198-.

Awards and Honors

Award for Excellence in Nursing Education; University of Maryland, 198-.

Selected Publications

Irving, Diana. "Clinical Competence of New Graduates: A Study to Measure Performance." The Journal of Continuing Education in Nursing (July/August, 198-).

Irving, Diana, and Lord, Phyllis. "The Technical Competence of Registered Nurses in the Administration of Oral Medications." The Journal of Nursing Education (1984).

Preparing a Letter of Introduction

The letter of introduction is an important adjunct to your CV or resumé. It gives you a chance to express your personal interest in a job or program in a way that the formats of the CV and resumé don't. Simply follow these guidelines:

1. Identify the specific person to whom you address the letter.
2. Identify key elements particular to the position involved.
3. Plan your letter; emphasize your interest and qualifications.
4. Write concisely and directly.
5. Type neatly; proofread carefully.

Identify the specific person. Invest in a phone call or a note, preferably the former, to the organization or institution involved. Ascertain the name of the person who is managing the selection process. Address your letter to that person. "To whom it may concern" is an absolute no-no.

Don't waste time on a letter to the president, director, chairperson of the board, or some other chief executive, unless that individual is the one managing the selection. Typically, the Chief will simply refer your note to the Indians anyway, and you will have lost time. Chief executive types are rarely involved at the screening level and often don't want to be bothered.

On the other hand, the manager of the selection and screening process may well be impressed that you took the time to discover that information.

Identify key elements. When you make the initial contact, request a job description, a list of qualifications, a statement of program goals, or whatever is available which enables you to learn exactly what the selectors are seeking. Make a list of the experiences, achievements, responsibilities, and talent which fit.

Plan. Make a list or write a draft; either way, feature your interest in the job and the particular merits you offer so that your most important assets are emphatic. Feature key elements from your list and clarify what elements of the situation especially appeal to you.

Write concisely. Never use four words when three will do, three when two will do, or two when one will do. If one is superfluous, eliminate it. A terse, direct letter will receive attention; a wordy, diffuse one will not. Say exactly what needs to be said in the fewest possible words. Feature brief sentences using active verbs and short, sharply focused paragraphs. Each major idea should be the subject of a paragraph. Several short, sharp paragraphs look better and read more easily than a long, involved one.

Type, proofread. A typed letter of introduction attracts little attention since it's what's expected. A handwritten letter, on the other hand, attracts unfavorable attention.

Proofread and correct your letter carefully. Typos, misspellings, and the like will kill you before you get to the interview stage.

Be sure that the format of your letter conforms with the standard format for a formal business letter.

Sample Letter of Introduction

0000 Moravia Avenue
Baltimore, MD 00000

Marie Marie, MSN
Chair, Search Committee
River Pediatric Hospital
303 Third Street
Kazoo, Michigan 11111

Dear Ms. Marie:

I write to express my interest in the Nursing Instructor position recently advertised.

As my resumé details, I have over seven years experience as a nursing instructor and a Master's in Nursing Education. I am especially interested in the curriculum development opportunities which the new position offers. My experience in curriculum design, both as a principal writer and as a committee member, prepare me well for such work.

I am prepared to appear for an interview at your convenience.

Respectfully,

Diana Irving

Selling Yourself Guidelines

1. Select and arrange all pertinent data for your CV.
2. Select only items which address the particular audience for your resumé.
3. Organize by date, moving backwards from the most recent, in CV and resumé.
4. Categorize items in CV and resumé.
5. Display categories and items in an easy to read format.
6. Develop items fully in your CV, briefly in your resumé, concisely in both.
7. Focus your resumé and letter of introduction directly on your intended audience.
8. Keep the resumé and letter of introduction brief and direct.
9. Type neatly.
10. Proofread!

Exercises

Exercise 1

Consult the want ads in a major metropolitan paper, such as the New York Times. Your library will have a copy. Select an advertisement for a job in your profession which is specific enough to help you focus. Prepare a resumé for that position.

Exercise 2

Solicit information regarding the above position. Prepare a letter of introduction accordingly.

Chapter 6
Writing for Publication

Objectives

After reading this chapter and completing the exercises, you should be able to prepare an article or book for publication.

Specifically, in this chapter you learn to:

- Brainstorm a potential article.
- Organize a sample paper for a particular audience.
- Write a sample query letter.
- Write a sample article.

Getting published is not nearly as difficult as many of us think it is. Certainly, the aura of being a "published author" exists. This aura carries, for some, a certain sense of awe. In fact, however, a publisher exists somewhere for nearly everything. If you wish to publish, you must simply find the proper vehicle.

Our intent in this chapter is to address the process of publishing in the health professions, specifically, the professional journals. Perhaps, given the specialization inherent in the various potential audiences, the generalization of a "publisher . . . somewhere for . . . everything" is less true. Finding that right vehicle to transport you to your intended audience may be the major challenge you face.

Like any other task, the challenge of writing for publication consists of a set of manageable parts. Approach the process systematically:

1. Clarify your idea.
2. Identify your audience.
3. Plan and organize.
4. Write a query letter.
5. Integrate "suggestions."
6. Write the paper.

In addition, we will consider how to handle the inevitable rejections which occur, and will also offer a few tips on dealing with textbook publishers.

Clarify Your Idea

An idea, like a child, needs a certain amount of nurturing to grow; your idea will not flourish left to itself. Different writers use different approaches, but here's an approach that works for many:

— Explore and brainstorm.
— Research and validate.

Explore and brainstorm. So you have a new idea. How can you get that idea out of your head and onto paper?

One way is to talk about it. Find a colleague who's knowledgeable and bounce your idea around. Capture ideas that seem interesting and save them. Don't be critical at this stage; grab any ideas that strike your fancy or seem even remotely useful.

Another way is to write down some key concepts which support or illustrate your idea. Just jot them down; forget about sequence at this point. Capture as many as you can.

If you have no sounding board and are unable to get ideas onto paper yet, use your tape recorder. Talk out some thoughts and play them back. If more ideas come, record them too. Let your thoughts flow freely.

Brainstorming like this tends to loosen up your thought process and get the creative juices flowing. The secret to success at this point is to be open to whatever ideas you generate. Capture them all. You can sort them later.

In addition, brainstorming helps you to focus. With a tentative focus in mind, you are better able to judge whether your idea is original and valid.

Research and validate. How original is your idea? Chances are that someone else has treated the same concept in some way or another. You need to know how others have addressed your idea so that you don't simply rework stale material. To find other articles, consult the periodical indices or use the medline. Chapter 8 explains how to use these resources.

Once you've located articles which address your topic, skim them, using the technique explained in chapter 8. Skimming will give you a very clear idea of the author's approach and treatment. If you feel that the article may have value for your potential audience, be sure to record the necessary bibliographical information. If you feel that the material might be useful to you, set up a note sheet and collect data for later reference.

Meanwhile, evaluate the originality and freshness of your idea. If you find that your point has been adequately treated both widely and recently, then you are probably wasting your time unless you can shape your idea so that you have something new to offer. Consider other possible applications of your idea. Perhaps you can address a new audience. Or maybe you can add a new angle or perspective to previous treatments. If not, this may be the time to abandon or shelve the idea.

As you review the literature, consider also whether your ideas are sound. Articles on the same topic will give you a frame of reference in which to operate. If your concepts contradict accepted views, be prepared to show why. Unsupported assertions are unlikely to satisfy an editor. Again, if your ideas are compatible with the literature, you must create a new feature of some kind in order to offer a contribution of value.

Now you have a reasonably clear idea not only of what you want to do, but also about what other writers have done with your topic.

Identify Your Audience

Before you plan your potential article in detail, you must decide exactly for whom you are writing. You have begun this process by researching your topic, familiarizing yourself with the periodicals which address the various audiences in the allied health professions.

Most likely, you will be writing for an audience whose goals and interests are like your own: you will have reviewed articles in journals which speak to you and others like you. If this is not the case, identify journals which are considered standard to your profession.

The title page of each journal gives a sense of that journal's intended audience, often in a phrase which follows the journal title—<u>ABC, The Journal for Alphabeticians</u>. This information tells you for whom the particular journal has been written. Now you must decide if your audience is that same group.

Decide if you are addressing students, new graduates, experienced practitioners, supervisors, managers, whomever. This decision rests on skills or knowledge one needs in order to understand the issues you will present. If the reader must have experienced a specific clinical setting or have mastered a specific skill, you should say so in your paper. Match your intended audience as best you can with that of a journal. Now you have a potential publisher in mind.

> <u>APPLICATION</u>:
> Generate an idea for a potential article. State the focus as clearly and specifically as possible. List potential audiences. List 2 journals which would be suitable publishers.

Plan and Organize

Planning your paper is likely to be easier now that you know generally what you want to say and to whom you wish to speak. Decide now, as specifically as possible, just what the purpose of your paper is. Write your purpose as clearly as you can. Ask yourself what ideas in your brainstorming list and from your literature review support your purpose. List these items.

Next decide what is the most effective order in which to present your discussion. Order of importance is a possibility when you are presenting data to support a point of view. If you are presenting a "how-to" paper, to explain a process or procedure, present your explanation step by step. Fit the sequence of the paper to the logic of the topic. Number the items on your list accordingly or rewrite the list in the order you've chosen. Be sure your list presents sufficient information for your intended audience. Refer to chapter 9 for more discussion of planning and organizing. At this point, you are ready to contact your potential publisher.

> APPLICATION:
> Plan the potential article whose focus you stated above.

Write a Query Letter

The first decision to make here is whether to write more than one initial query. Ethically, you should offer your paper to only one potential publisher at a time. If you decide to contact more than one publisher, indicate that you are doing so in your letter. You're better off, however, to query one journal at a time, allow 4-6 weeks for a response, and then move on to your second choice if you've heard nothing.

The query letter should be brisk and direct. Indicate your interest in the journal, state the major issue of your paper—refer to it as a paper, since it's not an article yet—and invite comments. Request a response at the editor's "earliest convenience."

Don't write a "dear editor" letter just yet. Each journal includes instructions about manuscript requirements and similar issues. You will also find a list of members of the editorial staff. Identify the acquisitions editor, if possible. Look on the contents page, and nearby, to locate the list of editorial staffers. Seek also, instructions as to how to submit materials. Frequently, journals publish a brief explanation of how to inquire of them. Some will say "We accept unsolicited manuscripts." Others will say flatly that they do not.

If the acquisitions editor is not identified, or if no instructions are available in the journal, then you'll be forced to write that "dear editor" letter. Address the editor in chief by name. That individual will refer your query to the right person.

Be sure your query is in the standard business letter format; use a good quality bond paper and type neatly. Enclose a resumé to establish your credentials. Be sure your letter describes the proposed paper succinctly, states your qualifications to write such a paper, and indicates the need for the paper. State the paper's proposed length and indicate whether you'll use tables, graphs, or other displays.

Sample Query

0000 Marriott Road
Marriott, MD 00000

Eve Adams, R.T.
Acquisitions Editor
Respiration Monthly
30 30th Street
Baltimore, MD 21000

Dear Ms. Adams,

I am preparing a paper discussing how to develop written procedures for various respiratory therapy techniques. Since Respiration Monthly frequently features materials for supervisors and in-service instructors, I believe this information might be useful. My paper presents the process of procedure development in small steps so that supervisors or instructors may prepare either actual procedures or instruction on procedures.

No other article on this topic has appeared in Respiratory Therapy journals in the last three years. Journal of Nursing, however, published my article on this topic, aimed, of course, at a nursing audience in September, 1983.

A detailed plan explaining the article and my resumé are enclosed. The article should run roughly nine pages double spaced. Two tables are included.

I await comments at your earliest convenience. The paper will be ready for review and suggestions within two weeks of your favorable response.

Respectfully,

John Gregory, Ph.D.

APPLICATION:
Write a sample query letter to one of the journals you've selected as a potential publisher.

Integrate Suggestions

Now wait. For the time being you are at the mercy of your potential publisher. By the way, forget about being paid. Chances are quite slim, since few professional journals pay for materials, and many which do offer only a token.

If you've heard nothing after 4-6 weeks, a note to the editor may be in order. Say you've heard nothing and wish to contact other journals. Allow another two weeks. At that point, if silence still prevails, write to your second choice. Then wait again.

If you receive a rejection note you can also go to your second choice. Sometimes the rejection contains a comment or two critiquing your proposal. If so, deal with these comments in your plan.

When your paper is accepted, your editor may wish you to make changes, major or minor. If the requested changes are unclear, or if you believe they alter your intent unacceptably, correspond with your editor to request clarification and perhaps to negotiate details of suggested changes.

Once you have finished with this process, integrate the suggestions into your plan. If you've already developed a draft, you'll now rewrite and revise accordingly. If you're working from a plan, as we suggest, simply revise the plan. If you wish further comment from your editor, submit the amended plan.

Write the Paper

Having reviewed the literature, planned the paper, and incorporated suggestions, you are just about ready to write. One more preliminary step is a good idea: analyze the style of presentation of your journal.

No two journals are exactly alike, but certain approaches tend to be in use. Many journals require an abstract, to be used as an introduction, and will specify which documentation format to use. Chapter 9 explains the two formats. Request specific guidance about which to use from your editor.

If no specific guidelines are forthcoming, simply review a few recent issues. Adopt the basic style you see. Many journals expect a condensed introduction, a body divided into key points labeled with subheadings, and a concise summary/conclusion.

If the journal style is unclear or eclectic, decide on your own how to proceed. Chapter 9 provides suggestions on beginnings, middles, and endings. We suggest the format above: an overview, a body subdivided and highlighted with headings, and a summary/conclusion. The overview should outline the major concepts of the paper; the body should follow point by point; the ending should recap. See the sample article at the end of this chapter for an example of how to organize a potential article.

Follow your plan, but not slavishly. Remember that, as you write, your ideas will develop further, so that some changes in your plan will inevitably occur. That's normal.

Before you send your paper in, give it a close reading and critiquing. Be sure it's complete, fully developed, and clearly organized.

How To Handle Rejection

You're not home free yet. Remember that your paper could still be rejected or could be accepted with revisions required. If the required revisions are acceptable, incorporate them. Otherwise, go to your second choice of publishers. At this point, if the journal accepts unsolicited manuscripts, go ahead and send the finished article, as is. Don't mention the previous rejection.

If you receive another rejection, don't panic. Simply send the paper out again, and hope. If you accrue a basket full of no's, consider reshaping the paper. To do so, go back to the clarifying stage and consider other possible ideas, audiences, and purposes.

How To Deal With Textbook Publishers

Dealing with textbook publishers is quite similar to dealing with journal publishers. In this instance, you'll follow the process above with one major difference: the product you offer is much larger. A minor difference is that selecting a publisher to query is not as easy as selecting a journal publisher.

Clarify your idea, identify your audience, plan and organize, write the query—now called a proposal—integrate suggestions, and write the book in the same sequence as you would an article. To find a textbook publisher suited to your audience, speak to colleagues and instructors, check the card catalogue in your library for texts addressing your audience, and consult your librarian. These sources will give some idea of which houses publish material for which markets.

Plan and organize the book in chapter format. Your book will probably need an introduction and several substantive chapters. The introduction should provide a detailed overview of the volume and should provide a frame of reference which gives the reader necessary background. Each chapter should contain a complete idea, and should be organized into recognizable beginning, middle, and ending. Selected readings or a glossary may be necessary depending on the intended audience. Plan accordingly. Offer exercises for readers if the text is intended for academic use.

Now write your proposal. Again, find out to which editor you should write and address that individual. Explain why your proposed text is unique. Present a terse purpose statement and an overview of the text. Include a detailed table of contents and a sample chapter, if possible. Be sure your target audience is clearly explicit. Include your CV with the proposal.

Wait. Handle suggestions as you would for a proposed article. Handle rejection similarly, too. Bear in mind that the proposal will circulate widely, so expect a long wait for a firm answer.

Decide, as you ponder, whether you want to write the book before you receive a positive response from an editor.

Your publisher will have specific requirements as to format, documentation, length, and the like. You may be forced to retype or otherwise generally alter your draft. Frequently, editors suggest additional chapters to engage a wider audience than you'd envisioned, so you'll need to expand your draft. At any rate, we advise that you get a commitment, if possible, before investing a great amount of time. Be prepared to make substantive changes in the text based on your editor's guidelines.

On the other hand, if you must write, do so. Just be prepared to rewrite extensively.

Once a publisher has accepted your idea, you will receive a publications manual of some type. Study it carefully, since it details all of the publisher's specific requirements. The publications manual also discusses the policy on obtaining permission to use other writers' material and on other legal and ethical issues. Avoid pitfalls by studying all of this before you get too far along. Review your plan at this point and negotiate suitable deadlines before you agree to a contract. Be sure the contract allows for renegotiation of deadlines.

Handle suggestions and write the book embodying your editor's wishes. The editor assigned to you probably understands your audience as well as you do and certainly understands marketing issues better than you do. As you write, structure chapters in parallel form, so that they all look and sound organizationally the same. Each has a beginning, a middle, and an end. Don't be afraid to make cross references to chapters. Many of your readers will read only selected chapters, so don't assume that you can build new ideas on previously presented ideas without saying so.

As with any writing task, writing a book is manageable in a set of small pieces. Approach the task accordingly.

Writing for Publication Guidelines

1. Before you write:
   - Clarify and focus your idea.
   - Identify your particular audience.
   - Plan carefully.
   - Send a terse query letter. Include a resumé and a plan.

2. As you write:
   - Integrate the comments and suggestions of your editor.
   - Follow your plan flexibly.

3. After you write:
   - Be prepared to revise and edit.
   - Be prepared to manage rejection.

Exercises

1. Brainstorm a list of points for your potential article.
2. Analyze the following sample article in terms of its organization: beginning, middle, ending; logically divide subparts.
3. Write a sample article, organized around a clear-cut beginning, middle, and ending. Divide the middle into its logical subparts and head them.

Sample Article

Job Analysis:
The Basis of Effective Appraisal
by Donna Ignatavicius and Jeff Griffith

Article Abstract: ***Required By Many Journals***

Job analysis identifies, specifies, organizes, and displays the duties, tasks, and responsibilities actually performed by the incumbent in a given job. These authors provide a comprehensive discussion of the job analysis process. They emphasize the importance of involving all levels in the analysis, from the chief nursing executive to the staff nurse. Their discussion will help you initiate and monitor a cooperative job analysis process to produce accurate job descriptions that clarify the institution's expectations and form the basis for effective performance appraisal.

Overview

Job analysis is the process of identifying, specifying, organizing, and displaying the duties, tasks, and responsibilities (DTRs) actually performed by the incumbent in a given job. When completed, the job analysis produces a job description that clarifies the institution's expectations and forms the basis for the incumbent's performance appraisal.

The benefits of the job analysis are several. First, the supervisor and worker develop a job description, which is neither a reflection nor an approximation of the job. The job description is the job; it defines the job precisely and therefore defines both supervisor's and worker's expectations. Second, because the process is cooperative, the participants initiate and continue open communication regarding effective job performance. Third, the consensus-based specificity of the job description minimizes the negative impact that subjectivity necessarily causes in appraisal. The task descriptions form the basic standards for measuring effectiveness.

Beginning the job analysis

Subhead:
To Focus The Reader's Attention

Somebody must be in charge of the job analysis, and we suggest that the chief nursing executive initiate and oversee the process. In fact, the best place to begin in job analysis is perhaps with the job of the chief nursing executive. Thereafter, the process is cooperative; from the top of the nursing department hierarchy to the bottom. The supervisors and the workers directly involved should perform the process together to reach consensus on each job description's accuracy. If each nurse from the staff level to the director level is directly involved, all participants feel a sense of ownership in the analysis and appraisal process.

Supervisory personnel for each unit—head nurse, team leader, assistant director—should manage and participate in the process in that unit. Individuals who actually do each job provide the data that the job analysis team, consisting of the supervisor and all unit members, molds into the job description. The entire process, from naming the job to preparing the job description is summarized in Exhibit 1.

EXHIBIT 1

1. Name the job.
2. List all duties, tasks, and responsibilities (DTRs) required or performed; survey incumbents; observe actual practice.
3. State all DTRs in behaviorally based terms; action verbs followed by direct objects are most effective.
4. Categorize duties according to purpose; categories might include direct care, maintenance, supervision, management, and interpersonal communication.
5. Prioritize duties within each category; prioritize categories.
6. Evaluate each DTR for specificity; no item should mix tasks, related or not.
7. Eliminate unnecessary items; rewrite unclear items.
8. Set standards for each DTR, develop a task analysis.
9. Identify constraints, such as the chain of command, and any experience requirements.
10. Summarize the job based on the proceeding analysis.
11. Prepare a job description in the following format:
    a) Job title
    b) Summary/overview
    c) DTRs by category and priority, including standards
    d) Constraints

Naming the job

A nurse is not necessarily a nurse. Although we use the same term, the duties of a staff nurse in obstetrics are different from those of a staff nurse in orthopedics, oncology, or ophthalmology. For the purposes of the job analysis, a generic job description for the position of staff nurse is possible as a base document, but supplementary descriptions are also needed to account for the unique characteristics of the staff nurse's responsibilities in a given unit. The final job description is individualized to fit the actual job, and the nurse who holds the job is oriented and evaluated according to particular duties.

Name the job specifically: staff nurse, obstetrics; team leader, orthopedics; assistant director of nursing, oncology. The job title should be a first clue to the exact nature of the job. Once the analysis is complete reconsider the title and make sure it still defines the job.

Listing all DTRs

Each job is a set of tasks whether they're called tasks, duties, or responsibilities. The term task refers to everything required in the performance of a given job. That includes everything the nurse does: supervisory and managerial duties, direct care tasks, maintenance tasks, interpersonal responsibilities, and anything else for which you hold the nurse accountable. In turn, do not hold the nurse accountable for anything not identified in the job description. Any additional task discussed in the performance evaluation should be included in the job description.

Develop the list of DTRs by surveying the incumbents in actual jobs. Ask them to list what they do; develop your own list and compare. Observe the employees in actual practice to verify the lists. Do not depend on existing job descriptions; isolate each specific task.

Supervisory, managerial, and interpersonal tasks are typically described by such generic statements as "provides clinical supervision to all staff as needed and assists in their development." This type of statement does not describe a task but rather a class of tasks. The category should be specified, but perhaps under managerial duties or under a separate class of tasks using the general statement as the heading. For example, in a team leader's job description, this category might include such specific items as:

> Identifies professional development
> needs of unit members.

Sets individual professional development goals cooperatively with unit members.

Monitors direct care delivery activities of unit members for conformity to hospital standards.

Instructs unit members in clinical skills when skill discrepancies occur.

If the lists of actual DTRs are incongruous, either at the staff level or between the supervisory and staff levels, then the job analysis team must reconcile the differences. If, for example, a variant task is important, perhaps each nurse should be responsible for it. If not, then perhaps it should be eliminated. Perhaps the task should be assigned to another job which might then be differently titled. For example, a task such as "make daily patient rounds with attending physicians and house staff" might be performed by the head nurse or the team leader. The team leader may think that this task is not actually her DTR, while the head nurse might feel that it is an appropriate DTR for the team leader. Perhaps both job descriptions (team leader and head nurse) should include this particular DTR, or perhaps it should be included in the job description for the supervisor or assistant director of nursing, and eliminated from the others. This is merely an example of a variant task and two ways in which the conflict, or variance could be handled.

When finished, the job analysis team should have a list representing a consensus of all involved.

Stating DTRs behaviorally

Once you identify what the nurse actually does, you must state it as clearly as possible so that you will know when the nurse is doing it. The behavioral mode is most effective. To state each task in behavioral terms, use action verb phrases. For example, a required task for a team leader might once have been stated, "is responsible and accountable for the follow through of physician's orders." This statement is not only unclear but also wordy. The wording should capture the intent of the task and describe the overt behavior. "Is responsible" does not describe overt behavior and therefore the behavior cannot be identified and evaluated. The intent, might be worded "directs the implementation of physician's orders," but this revised statement, though concise, may not be sufficiently precise. A qualifying phrase would be necessary to explain the task; for example, the task may be "directs the implementation of physician's orders by assigning patient care to specific staff members" and "by observing the patient care process."

Now the task is specific and clear. What the nurse does and how the nurse does it are specified with an action verb and expanded with qualifying phrases. Each task must be carefully worded by keeping these principles in mind.

Categorizing DTRs

Job descriptions typically mix varied tasks illogically, and the result is a confusing miscellany. When this happens, neither the incumbents nor their supervisors have a clear sense of the dimensions of the job. To avoid this problem, classify tasks by type. A team leader's job is likely to include managerial and supervisory tasks, direct case tasks, maintenance tasks, and interpersonal tasks.

For a team leader, managerial and supervisory tasks might include "directs the implementation of physician's orders." Direct care tasks would include such hands-on patient care tasks as "takes and records vital signs." Maintenance tasks might include "orders supplies" and interpersonal tasks would include "teaches patients about medication regimen." A single task should belong in only one category. For example, "initiates and directs the development of patient care plans" is poorly phrased as a two-part task. If the team leader both "initiates" and "directs," then "initiates development of patient care plans" belongs under direct care tasks, while "directs development of patient care plans" belongs under managerial and supervisory tasks. If tasks are stated succinctly in behavioral terms, categories should not overlap.

Once you have a consensus about tasks, derive categories based on your list of DTRs. Do not force tasks into preconceived classifications. The purpose of categorizing tasks is to design a structure that provides a logical framework. Some institutions have developed categories such as "duties to patients," "duties to peers," "duties to the institution," and "duties to self." Custom design your job descriptions to meet your own needs.

Prioritizing DTRs

For a given job, one specific category of tasks is likely to be most important. For example, the top priority for a "team leader" might be managerial and supervisory tasks. For a staff nurse, the priority is probably direct care tasks. Priorities, of course, will vary depending on the job and the institution. The job description should list tasks by priority within each category.

Set priorities by consensus. The supervisor and worker must decide together, using hospital philosophy and policy as a guide but considering above all the needs of the unit and its patients. When setting priorities is difficult because tasks are regarded as equally important, make a forced choice. Resolve these disputes at the staff level whenever possible, but remember that the ultimate decision about priorities rests with the chief nursing executive.

Prioritizing also demonstrates the values of the tasks performed. Both the nurse and the supervisor thereby know what is most important and what is least important. The agreed-upon priorities also help the nurse make day-to-day decisions, for when the nurse must choose between two tasks, the most important is predetermined. During a performance appraisal, priority tasks receive greatest attention.

Job descriptions that do not organize tasks coherently contribute to inefficient performance and performance appraisals that focus undue attention on trivial elements. Job descriptions that do organize tasks coherently help nurses manage their time efficiently.

Evaluating for specificity

At this point, evaluate the list of DTRs to be certain that each DTR states the intent of the task exactly. When necessary, this statement should also explain how or when the task is performed. For example, "takes and records vital signs" should be qualified by "every shift" in some units, by "every four hours" in others, or by "daily" in yet others. "Teaches patients about medication regimen" could be qualified by "at the time of discharge" and by "using the standard hospital protocol for patient teaching." Such qualifiers not only provide direction but also provide the basis for setting standards.

Specific statements clarify performance expectations. Clear expectations provide the basis for employee appraisal, employee development, and employee training and orientation. The action verb of the item is the "what;" qualifiers provide the "where," "when," "how," or "why,"

Be wary of qualifiers like "as needed," unless the need is specifically defined. Need is a discrepancy between what is and what should be. Thus, whenever actual performance differs from desired performance, a need exists. The need in "teaches patients about medication regimen" is the patient's inability to identify the frequency, action, and side effects of the drugs. The need in "instructs unit members in clinical skills when skill discrepancies occur" is a skill discrepancy. A staff member who fails to follow an isolation procedure needs direction in when, how, or why to initiate or maintain isolation. Once the need is stated specifically, you can readily determine the precise qualifiers.

Precision also means separating individual tasks, even if they are related, unless they are actually parts of a single process. For example, "initiates and/or directs the development of patient care plans" is part of a task statement in a team leader's job description. But which is it to be? Initiate? Direct? "And/or" further clouds the issues. If the team leader does both, then the job description should say so, should place the tasks in their appropriate categories, and should say when, why, or how. Stated specifically, the two tasks are "initiates development of patient care plans" and "directs development of patient care plans." "And/or" is the crutch of crippled thought.

The familiar "performs other duties as required" is useless. If "other duties" are important, identify and state them in their priority relationship. If they are not important, eliminate the item. When you can think of no way to avoid "other duties," at least include examples, such as "performs other duties such as . . . when . . . ." Better yet, include a statement in the institution's policy manual to define types of "other duties" and the situations in which they are typically to be performed. This is a step toward specifying these duties; it leaves room for clarification in the future.

Eliminating and rewriting

Now review the analysis with the job analysis team. Does the list of tasks, as determined by consensus, contain items that are not really part of the job? For example, can team leaders in nursing service realistically "serve as public relations liaison with the larger hospital community?" Such items might include the puffery sometimes used to inflate a job's importance, but it's more likely that they include low priority tasks that are more properly assigned to other personnel.

The remaining items comprise the job as it exists in the real world. To check each task for clarity, share the analysis with each worker or supervisor who has a stake in it. When each of them can state the intent of a task to the satisfaction of the others, the statement is clear.

Setting standards

Setting standards is more complex than we can discuss fully here, but the job analysis team has already completed the most important part of this step by isolating and naming the tasks. Statisticians call this process nominal measurement, and the same principle applies here. Until you name a desired performance, you cannot measure it by counting it.

If the task statement is so clear that you will be able to distinguish desired performance from all other performance, you have a measurement of performance. The next step is to decide how often or in what ratio of possible situations the performance should occur. To decide this, simply ask yourself, "how does a person whom I consider competent perform under relatively normal circumstances?" In statistical terms, this performance provides a referent that establishes a baseline for evaluating performance. In some cases, such as taking and recording vital signs, the referent may be 100 percent accuracy at all times. Another standard of performance might be "writes care plans for 80 percent of assigned patients using the hospital guidelines for care plan construction." Set the standard to reflect reality. Review your standards periodically with the assistance of those who will be judged by them.

In some cases, a task analysis of the desired performance may be necessary to define the task with sufficient clarity. A task analysis is a step-by-step procedure much like a job analysis. Analyses of certain tasks probably exist in your procedure manual. Review these for accuracy and use them as the basis for performance standards where they can provide adequate guidance; where they do not, or where they do not exist, perform a task analysis as follows to develop revised or new procedures.

1. State task as clearly as possible.
2. List all steps necessary to complete the task. Check to be sure they are in sequence.

3. State each step with an action verb.
4. Review the steps.
    a. Check their sequence.
    b. Eliminate unneeded steps.
    c. Verify their completeness.
    d. Identify substeps, if any.
5. Identify pitfalls and facilitators.

Task analysis may be accomplished by performing, observing, or simulating the task, or by brainstorming. The most effective mode for analyzing technical tasks is observing an especially competent practitioner. The observer asks the questions and records the process so that items are listed behaviorally under a heading reading "do this." Watch for pitfalls and facilitators. The observer considers what could go wrong at each step and builds in a protective action. Another consideration: "Is there a way to perform this step that will facilitate the process?" If so, the observer builds that in too.

For interpersonal tasks and some managerial and supervisory tasks, brainstorming is the most effective analysis mode. For example, if a DTR is "cooperates with other units in coordinating patient care," the best approach is to bring everyone who has this responsibility together and develop a list by consensus of behavioral descriptions that define the task. Once the list is complete, prioritize the descriptions.

The task analyses and numerical standards are not usually displayed in the job description because doing so would produce job descriptions of forbidding bulk. Your institution's policy manual is the place to publish this information. Just make sure that supervisors and workers have access to clear statements of expected performance as a touchstone against which to compare actual performance and as a basis for training and orientation.

Identifying constraints

How does the job fit into the overall framework of the institution? To whom does the incumbent report? Is the job category unionized? What is the pay scale? What experience and training are required? These are the constraints on the job. Include a list of these factors in the job description; omit nothing that is necessary to place the job in its institutional relationship.

Summarizing the job

Now that you have analyzed the job thoroughly, you are prepared to write a succinct overview. Its purpose is to provide a frame of reference as an introduction to the job description. Use this summary to focus attention on the unique facets of the job; use it to capture the job's flavor. When supervisors and workers have read the summary, they will be prepared to read the list of DTRs intelligently.

Preparing a job description

Conclusion: ***Summarizes Key Ideas In The Article***

Finally, write the actual job description based on your analysis. First present the individual job title. Next present the overview. If several jobs are similar, as with the job of staff nurse on various units, prepare a generic description that isolates the common elements; then develop individual addenda for each job. This procedure will eliminate the need to produce infinite numbers of descriptions. Next list the DTRs, stated behaviorally, by category and priority. Again, where several related jobs are the same, combine them in a generic model and individualize by use of addenda. Include at the end a statement of the constraints. Exhibit 2, a partial example of a job description for team leader on a medical-surgical unit, includes several possible categories and DTRs under each, as well as a list of constraints.

EXHIBIT 2

This Exhibit Provides A Sample of the Desired Product

PARTIAL SAMPLE OF JOB DESCRIPTION

Team Leader; Medical/Surgical Unit

I. Overview:

The Team Leader directs team members in delivering patient care.

The Team Leader assesses, plans, implements, and evaluates care for assigned patients.

II. Duties, Tasks, Responsibilities

A. Supervisory:

Monitors direct care delivery activities of team members for conformity to hospital standards.

Plans patient assignments for team members.

Identifies professional development needs of team members.

Sets individual professional development goals cooperatively with team members.

B. Direct Care:

Assesses patients' needs upon admission in cooperation with team.

Initiates the development of patient care plans in conformance with hospital standards.

Monitors patient progress related to care plan.

Evaluates nursing care related to care plan and hospital standards.

Provides patient care when insufficient staffing and patient needs dictate.

C. Interpersonal:

Informs team members of patient status.

Informs team members of changes in policies, procedures, and standards.

Identifies conflicts among team members and initiates solutions.

Reports patient status to other shifts.

D. Educational:

Instructs team members in clinical skills when skill discrepancies occur.

Orients new employees to hospital policies and procedures, to team function, and to facility layout.

III. Constraints:

The Team Leader:
is an R.N.,
has at least two year's experience,
is an exempt employee in salary category 2,
reports to the Head Nurse.

Remember to perform job analysis in concert with the workers and supervisors who will use the job descriptions. The best way to ensure clarity is to build consensus. The cooperation atmosphere that results from consensus is the basis for effective management and performance appraisal.

Chapter 7
Writing Memoranda and Letters

Objectives

After reading this chapter and completing the exercises, you should be able to prepare clear, straightforward memos and letters more effectively and efficiently.

Specifically, in this chapter you learn to:

- Focus clearly on your message.
- Identify your audience and its needs.
- Organize your ideas.
- Present your message attractively and accessibly.
- Emphasize your main points.
- Rewrite and revise for clarity and consciseness.

Memo and letter writing should be the simplest writing tasks that any of us face. That they are not may be the result of inattention, haste, or even apathy—who knows? The result is that memoranda and letters are often overly long, diffuse, unclear, and confusing. In this chapter we aim to present a straightforward system for writing memos and letters that will not only save time but will also enhance results.

Memoranda and letters tend to be of two types: action or information. The action type asks its audience to do something; the information type explains or provides data which the writer believes will be useful or interesting to the audience.

If your communication is an action item, you must make your expectations absolutely clear to the reader. What do you expect the reader to do? Why? When? How?

If your communication is an information item, you must condense and summarize the information as concisely and clearly as possible. What is the precise point?

Approach memo and letter writing this way:

1. Determine focus and purpose.
2. Identify the intended audience.
3. List and organize key points to be presented.
4. Design a suitable format.
5. Condense and simplify.

Determine Focus and Purpose

The first issue to consider in any writing task is "What is the point?" In preparing an effective memo or letter, this question is especially important, since a sharp focus is critical to conciseness. The more clearly you zero in on the point you wish to address, the better.

Create a single focus; otherwise you obscure the issue. If the point you address consists of a series of interrelated ideas, summarize the general point and then present the subpoints. The overall point must be clear, or the subpoints will make no sense. For example, if you are transmitting a report for analysis and comment, state the major issue and then call attention to supporting ideas which require analysis. If you must address several unrelated major issues, you should probably write several separate communications, each with a precise point.

If you require a response, say so, and set a deadline. Specify the type of response required and when it is needed. You might expect a phone call; on the other hand, you might provide a tear-off or return post card if you need a written response. Many agencies include return post cards requiring only a check mark—Yes, I'm coming; No, I'm not—and a signature. This technique costs a few pennies, but virtually guarantees results.

If you send attachments or addenda, be sure to allude to them in your text and explain their importance. Perhaps you expect analysis or comment. Say so. Do not include such materials unless absolutely necessary.

The same thing goes for the oft-abused P.S. If the postscript were really important, it would be in the text. If a reiteration of something in the text, the P.S. is redundant. In either case, the P.S. is ineffective and distracting. Use it very sparingly and only when you have no alternative.

Focus on a single issue: zero in precisely and you can reduce misunderstanding while you eliminate verbosity.

APPLICATION:

1. State the point of an action memo; identify the action required and the deadline.
2. State the point of an information letter. If you just summarize a general idea, list major subpoints as well.

Identify the Intended Audience

You may be addressing a single individual, a large crowd or any combination in between. Whatever the case, you can be sure that your audience is very busy, highly distracted, and maybe even disinterested. Your challenge is to find a way to appeal to an audience which, consciously or unconsciously, resists your best efforts.

Another important strategy is to limit your audience. If you are circulating an information memo, restrict circulation to those who really need the material. If you are writing a letter of complaint, send it to the person who can help you. Resist the temptation to send copies to half the people in the hemisphere. You'll annoy the person who can help and bemuse those who can't. In such cases, you may need to make some phone calls or otherwise research the chain of command, but this activity is most likely to produce results.

Consider also that overuse of memoranda or letters diminishes their effectiveness. If you get the reputation of being a memo machine or a letter factory, your communications will end up in the trash can without being read. Restrict your correspondence to issues which are demonstrably necessary.

Evaluate your method of circulation as well. Some agencies habitually post communications on bulletin boards and leave them thereon forever. The symbolic message is that the content of these aging missives is unimportant. If the most efficient way to circulate a memo or letter is to post it, select a specific, highly accessible and visible place. Clear the area of old materials on a fixed schedule, say every ten days. Be sure to announce this procedure to all involved. If you need to be sure that certain individuals see the message, request that they sign or initial the document.

Another technique is to route a message from person to person by attaching a routing sheet with each member of the intended audience listed and a timeline specified. Each recipient reads the message, initials in the assigned spot, and passes the material to the next person listed.

Most importantly, whatever your focus, writing style, or mode of dissemination, be sure to consider one essential issue before you write. Ask yourself, "What does my audience need to know?" Limit your communication to that issue and send your message only to those who need to hear it.

APPLICATION:

1. Identify the recipient(s) of your action memo. Limit circulation to the essential persons.
2. Identify the recipient(s) of your information letter. Limit circulation likewise.

List and Organize Key Points

So far you've clarified the focus of your communication and identified your intended audience. Now you are ready to organize your thoughts logically and develop them fully.

First, make a list of the key elements you must address. Next, number the items in the order of their importance. Finally, list under each item the detail needed to assure clarity.

Let's consider an example. We'll start from scratch with an action letter.

Focus: The meeting and agenda of the sexual abuse work group
Audience: Members of the work group.

Key elements:	***Details:***
1. Time	2:30-4, May 2, 198-.
2. Place	Rm. 300A, Admin. Bldg, County General.
3. Tentative Agenda	Minutes. Introduction of guests. Education Committee Report. Treatment Committee Report.
4. Agenda Items Needed	Submit by 5/15/8-.
5. Materials Needed	Calendars. Copies of committee reports from Chairpersons.
6. RSVP Required	Phone me by 5/15/18-.

Such a plan constitutes a skeletal draft of your communication and assures focus and clarity. Note that the details help the audience prepare for the meeting by establishing start and end times, reminding committee chairs to provide copies of reports, and setting deadlines for agenda items and RSVP. Recipients now have a structure within which to plan. Meeting the needs of your audience helps assure effectiveness.

Now, let's consider another example. Here's a plan of a letter requesting information:

Focus: Need data on recovery rates of abuse victims for research project.
Audience: Adams, M.S.W., Director of Counseling, State Hospital.

Key points:	***Details:***
1. Purpose of Study	Compare traditional 1-1 counseling with family counseling.
2. Specific Data Needed	Number of clients served. Type of counseling provided. Length of treatment. Recidivism.
4. Deadlines	Respond by 3/1/8-. Report due 5/1/8-.
3. Response Required	Data sheet enclosed with stamped self-addressed envelope.

Note here that the plan forestalls the kind of unfocused communication which yields negative results. The typical letter of this type asks for "any information you can send me." That request elicits either no response at all, a mound of unsifted paper that probably doesn't include the needed data, or an invitation to visit and search the files yourself.

A note on style: Use short, outline format statements or terse sentences in your plan. These parts build easily into crisp, direct sentences.

Here's a final example, an action memo:

Focus: Changes in procedure resulting from new law: recommendations.
Audience: Members of Standards Committee.

Key Points:	***Details:***
1. Public Law 98-100	Requires performance based education, individualized rating forms, periodic job analysis, and merit pay. Implementation deadline 12/31/8-.
5. Attachment	Copies of law.
2. Action Requested	Specific suggestions on how to implement.
3. Response Required	Memo or letter.
4. Deadline	6/8/8-.

To organize logically and develop effectively, you need simply to ask "What does my audience need to know?" and list those points in their order of importance. The few seconds you invest in designing this plan will pay dividends by saving time with the actual writing and by producing enhanced results. For example, you'll have fewer questions to answer from persons who don't understand your point.

APPLICATION:
1. Plan your action memo.
2. Plan your information letter.

Design a Suitable Format

For most letters, the standard business letter format is best. Your return address and phone number are on the upper right, your correspondent's address is on the left. You remember; you learned this in third grade. You'd be surprised, however, to learn how many writers request a response but neglect to provide information about where to respond. Then, no doubt, they grumble about the rude person who didn't have the courtesy to respond.

The formal business letter format is very simple. The sample letters in this chapter and in chapters five and six are examples. If you need details on spacing or variant formats, check your library for a professional typist's manual.

In the body of your letter use short sentences and paragraphs to highlight key points. Short paragraphs are particularly effective, in that they use white space to focus attention.

For memos, commercial forms are readily available, but a plain homemade format will usually do. Such a format should emphasize focus, audience,and certain key points.

Example:

To:
From:
Subject:
Action Required:
Deadline:

Again, use short sentences and paragraphs to emphasize major elements in the body of your message.

If your message requires wide circulation or frequent reuse, you'll need to produce numerous copies—a "form" letter or memo. As you know, form letters or memoranda receive less attention than those which are personalized. If you have access to a word processor, personalizing is no problem. Otherwise, you may wish to consider alternative approaches. For example, a copied letter with the individual recipient's name typed in and a personal signature is less offensive than straight copy. Most of us don't expect personalized memos, but tend to react positively when our names are written on the copy and the sender has initialed the copy. In some cases, a brief handwritten note on the copy is an effective personalized touch. At any rate, consider your audience and assess the impact of an impersonal correspondence. If the form letter could do damage, find a way to personalize.

APPLICATION:

1. Design a format for your action memo.
2. Design a format for your information letter.

Condense and Simplify

Now you are ready to write. Follow your plan but don't do so slavishly. Present each point in the order you've determined, including supporting detail. As you proceed, if you discover that your planned sequence isn't working, don't be afraid to change. The first draft you produce is really only a trial run anyway, so expect to make changes.

Keep your communication brief, your sentences short and direct, and your word choices simple. As you write, concentrate on short sentences in short paragraphs. No law says that a one sentence paragraph designed to emphasize an important point is a capital offense. The longer your letter or memo, the less likely your audience will read it. The longer a sentence, the more difficult to understand; the more multisyllabic, specialized, or high flown a word choice, the more likely to put off or annoy your reader.

Select simple, direct words that say exactly what you mean. Resist the temptation to obscure your message with edubabble, psychobabble, medicojargon, or multisyllabic terms for which precise one syllable synonyms exist. Your goal is not to impress your audience with your education, but rather to convey a clear message.

If you realize, as you write, that a given item in your plan is unneeded, eliminate it. If an item is redundant, do the same. The result will be athletic, lean communication.

Remember to review the first draft of your effort. Correct typographical, spelling, or grammatical errors. Eliminate superfluous or redundant materials. Clarify unclear points.

As you revise, eliminate passive voice verb constructions and wordiness. The exercises at the end of this chapter address this issue.

Finally, share your draft with a colleague and get a second opinion. If the communication is important enough, this small bit of extra time will pay off. A second reader often spots problems which we miss.

Now, let's consider a sample or two. Here's the action memo we planned earlier.

Sample Memo

To: Members of the Sexual Abuse Work Group

From: Helen Arbutus, Chair

Subject: Meeting, 5-20-8-, 2:30-4:00 P.M.
Place: Room 300A, Administration Building, County General, 100 Elm Street

If you wish to submit agenda items, please do so by 5-15-8-. The tentative agenda includes:

Minutes
Introduction of guests
Education Committee report
Treatment Committee report

Be sure to bring your calendars. Committee chairs should provide copies of reports.

Please let me know if you plan to attend by 5-15-8- on 555-0000, ext. 0.

Note that this memo labels certain key information so that the reader cannot become confused. Additional information appears in short sentences, clustered in short paragraphs. Spacing and white space help highlight these points. An alternative would be to label these points as well.

Here's a second example, the letter requesting information—a type of action letter—planned earlier.

Sample Letter

J Jones
0000 Oak Place
Baltimore, Maryland 00000
555-1111

January 1, 198-

R. L. Adams, MSW
Director of Counseling
State Hospital Center
0000 Avenue A
Philadelphia, Pennsylvania 00000

Dear Ms. Adams,

I am conducting a study on the effectiveness of traditional one-on-one counseling compared to family counseling. In order to develop a sufficient data base, I need your help.

Could you provide me with the following information?

1. Types of counseling provided.
2. Numbers of clients served in each.
3. Average length of treatment in each.
4. Recedivism rate for clients in each.

Please use the data sheet enclosed and return in the stamped, self-addressed envelope provided.

Since my report is due on May 8, 198-, I'll need your response by March 1, 198-.

If you have any questions, please call me collect. My office hours are 1:00 P.M.-3:30 P.M. daily.

Thanks for your help. If you'd like a copy of the report, just check the box on the data sheet.

Respectfully,

Jean Jones

Note that this letter is direct and straight-forward. The sentences are crisp; the paragraphs focused.

APPLICATION:
1. Prepare your action memo using the plan and format you've developed.
2. Prepare your information letter using the plan and format you've developed.

Memo/Letter Writing Guidelines

1. Focus clearly on a particular issue.
2. Specify what response or results you need, how, and by when.
3. Analyze your precise audience and its needs.
4. List and organize key points ***before*** you write.
5. Present your message in a format which highlights major items and presents each point accessibly.
6. Revise and rewrite: condense and simplify, eliminating redundancy, wordiness, vagueness.

Exercises

Exercise 1

Prepare a memo announcing a meeting. Be sure to include where and when, as well as whatever information or materials participants will need when they arrive.

Exercise 2

Prepare a letter requesting information. Identify the person who can provide the information and specify precisely what you need.

Exercise 3

Revise the following. Use active voice. Eliminate wordiness.

a. It is recommended that we consider the following.
b. The reason this approach is proposed is because of its efficiency.
c. It is the responsibility of each individual to maintain a professional image of the profession.
d. In addition to the current practice of one-on-one encounters with various team members, group classes are being planned.
e. It is important that the patient assessment be made on all patients prior to their referral for classes.
f. An area that has not been explored is that of specific resource people, i.e., a podiatrist.
g. The tubing is longer in length.
h. Any questions regarding the new protocol are to be referred to Jeff Griffith.
i. The spaces on the data sheet are to be filled in with the time, drug, dose, route of administration, and/or any vital signs on procedures.
j. Specific criteria have been developed to describe expected behaviors at each level.
k. Attached please find a copy of the evaluation summary report.

Unit III
Writing in the Academic Setting

Introduction

Graduate or undergraduate, students know that the bane of their existence is the so-called "term paper." Actually, the phrase is a misnomer, since hardly anyone ever uses an entire term to write one, but never mind. The two chapters which follow attempt to simplify "term paper" writing, the process of performing secondary research and presenting your findings.

Chapter 8, "Conducting Secondary Research," explains the process of developing a topic, locating sources, and taking notes. Chapter 8 also explains how to prepare a precis, which is a form of an abstract. Here, using research and note-taking concepts gleaned from the preceeding discussion, you learn how to summarize and condense information in order to present a concise precis of materials you've studied. You'll notice, we hope, that note-taking and condensing will be useful to you as study skills.

Chapter 9, "Planning and Writing the Secondary Research Paper," flows directly from Chapter 8, explaining how to plan, organize, prepare, and document the paper. In this chapter, we attempt to take the pain out of reference notes and bibliographies.

Chapter 8 displays sample research notes and precis; Chapter 9 two sample papers. Again, these examples should help you see concretely what your product will be. Each chapter also offers exercises to help you practice the concepts you've learned. We hope these chapters will be especially useful to readers who are returning to school, seeking advanced degrees, or simply taking courses for self improvement.

Chapter 8
Conducting Secondary Research

Objectives

After reading this chapter and completing the exercises, you should be able to carry out secondary research.

Specifically, in this chapter you learn to:

- Use periodical indices, medline, and card catalogue.
- Select and focus a topic for research writing.
- Skim research sources effectively.
- Avoid common pitfalls in doing secondary research.
- Prepare research notes.
- Write a precis.

"To produce a good research paper is a thoroughly satisfying experience," says Audrey Roth, author of The Research Paper (vii). "Oh No! Not another term paper!" groans the beleaguered student. Why is the "term paper" such a plague on students? Can research writing become bearable? The approach one takes to any writing task produces the pain or pleasure, so let's consider how to make the research paper satisfying.

"Term Papers" have been a blight on many of us. This chapter and the next take a stab at making secondary research more friendly. Our focus in Chapters 8 and 9 will be on the secondary research paper or term paper, that is, one based on secondary sources: more about the distinction between primary and secondary research later.

In this chapter, we'll take a detailed look at a step by step process for performing the research in preparation for writing a secondary research paper; then, in the last section of this chapter, we'll see how to develop a precis. In the next chapter, we'll consider the actual procedure for writing the paper itself.

Remember that the purpose of the research paper is not to read untold numbers of encyclopedia articles and to regurgitate them in mindlessly parrot-like tones. Rather, the purpose is to learn about a topic in which you are interested and to present what you have learned to your audience. If you use the research process to expand your knowledge of something you need or want to know, then your burden lightens.

First, approach the job systematically. Any big job is no more than a series of little jobs. Preparing a research paper, while seemingly monumental, is really only a step by step process. Deal with one step at a time, something like this:

1. Identify potential topics.
2. Select potential sources.
   a. secondary.
   b. primary.
3. Gather background information.
4. Narrow the focus.
5. Skim the sources.
6. Note useful information.

In many cases, you will actually be doing several steps concurrently, but the process consists of these pieces and is manageable in small parts as long as you don't get bogged down. Notice that the process involves planning and organizing long before writing takes place. Time in planning saves time overall. Because this chapter deals with each of the steps separately, you should read the entire chapter before you apply any of the individual steps. All the steps are interrelated.

Identify Potential Topics

Focus your efforts on a topic which reinforces, expands, or complements your professional goals, your interests, or your needs. For example, if you are studying to be a dietitian, select a topic which relates to your studies, such as the role of a certain food or spice in contributing to stress or hyperactivity. If you are interested in a particular specialty, say pediatrics, select a topic which relates to that specialty, such as control of attention deficit disorder (hyperactivity) through diet or the relationship between diet and learning. If you are working with a client who is hypertensive, select a topic related to managing the condition through diet. That is, shape the research assignment to suit you. When you are assigned a topic, especially a general one, rework it. "Stress," for example, can become "Managing Stress Through Diet."

Your range of potential topics reflects your interests, goals, and concerns. Try to avoid writing about topics which have no relationship to your situation, personal, academic, or professional. Make a list of possibilities and rank them in order of preference. Now when you begin to look for information you'll have some idea of how to proceed.

Identify Potential Sources

Once you have a topic or two in mind, you are ready to begin gathering information. Obviously, your topic and your level of experience will dictate which sources are most useful to you.

Here we focus on the process of conducting secondary research, research, that is, which relies on data already collected, analyzed, and reported by others in texts, journals, and other media. Primarily research relies on original investigation through observation, experiment, analysis, survey, and a variety of other techniques of gathering data first hand. Of course, you may wish to use a first hand case study to supplement your secondary work—perhaps you can report on a patient or client—but the process of conducting primary research is the subject of another book.

If your topic is unfamiliar or if you have little experience doing research, you may want to begin by consulting a medical dictionary or encyclopedia in order to get a definition of key terms and some general background on your topic. Formal definitions may even be useful for well informed writers.

For example, suppose you are assigned the topic "Cerebrovascular Accident." Dox, Melloni, and Eisner will tell you that cerebrovascular refers to the blood supply to the brain (91), and that an accident is an "unexpected, sudden, undesirable event, or an unforseen complication" (4). Under the entry for accident, you'll find that cerebrovascular or cerebralvascular accident is an "occlusion or rupture of a blood vessel in the brain; also called stroke or apoplexy" (91). The value of the dictionary is to help you to build a frame of reference which is useful in getting started.

Periodical indices. Next, you'll consult the indices to periodicals which feature articles aimed at your profession. Cumulative Index to Nursing and Allied Health Literature (CINAHL), Hospital Literature Index (HLI), and Index Medicus (IM) are the most useful for you.

In some instances, Education Index and Social Sciences Index may also prove useful. All of these indices are available at your college or university library. Since the latter two are not quite so specialized as the medically oriented indices, they are likely to be available in your local library, too.

Each of these indices intends to reach a specific audience. If, for the purposes of your research assignment, you are part of that audience, seek out the apropos index:

CINAHL indexes 300 nursing, allied health, and health related journals. Published five times yearly, CINAHL is aimed specifically at nurses and allied health professionals, including cardiopulmonary technology, emergency services, health education, medical and lab technology, medical assistant, medical records, occupational therapy, respiratory therapy, physical therapy and rehabilitation, radiologic technology, and social service in health care. The principal focus of CINAHL is patient care related issues. Each year, CINAHL publishes a cumulative volume.

HLI indexes over 500 journals, focusing on materials related to hospital and health facility administration, health planning, and administrative aspects of health care delivery. Article coverage includes the delivery of health care in settings such as hospitals, health centers, health maintenance organizations, homes for the aged, hospices, mobile units, nursing homes, occupational health facilities, and rehabilitation centers. The emphasis of coverage includes topics such as organization and management; clinical equipment, physical plant, and furnishings, and the effects of new technology; health planning; health care education; financial management and cost effectiveness; facility planning and construction; legislation, regulation, and accreditation; personnel management; patient care services; quality assurance; and risk management. Articles on clinical aspects of patient care are excluded; such articles are indexed in CINAHL. HLI also publishes a cumulative volume each year.

IM indexes biomedical journal materials. Its primary audience is physicians, but other allied health professionals will find IM useful, in that its citations include 117 English language journals. IM includes directions on use in the front of each issue, along with sample entries for interpretation. Articles in IM are given under those multi ple subject headings representing the central concepts. A full citation appears in each reference.

Entries in the indices vary in form. Hypothetical samples are displayed and interpreted below. CINAHL and HLI index by both subject heading and author.

CINAHL:

Article title, all lower case — Preparing the comprehensive patient care plan (Irving, D. et al)
Major Author's name, in parenthesis
Journal Title, all caps — NURSE MAG 1983 Oct/Nov 21 121-5
Year and month of publication
Volume
Page numbers

When the article title is too vague to clarify its focus for the reader, CINAHL's indexers add descriptors. Subject headings frequently have subdivisions as well, and cross referencing places some articles under multiple headings.

HLI:

Journal Title, lower case, dark type
Article title, lower case — Comprehensive health planning
Author's name — Gregory, J. **Respiratory Mag**
Year and month of publication 1983 Oct-Nov.: 21(4) : 126-32
Volume and number
Page numbers

HLI also indexes articles under multiple headings when helpful to do so.

IM:

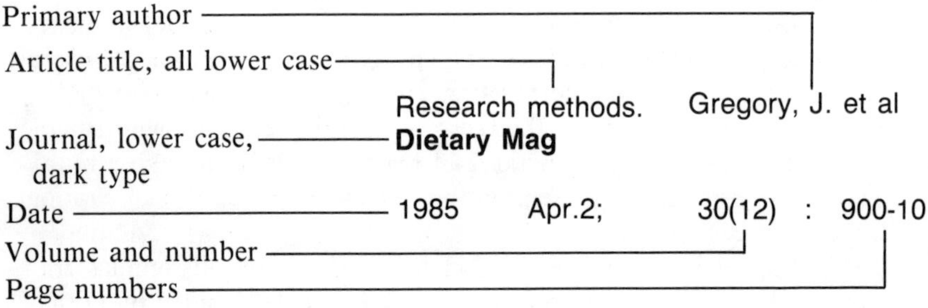

Primary author				Gregory, J. et al
Article title, all lower case	Research methods.			
Journal, lower case, dark type	**Dietary Mag**			
Date	1985	Apr.2;		
Volume and number			30(12)	
Page numbers			:	900-10

Note that though the exact format on entries varies slightly, CINAHL, HLI, and IM present article data in the same order: article title, author, journal title abbreviation, date of issue, volume, and inclusive page numbers.

Use the indices not only to locate but also to screen potential sources. Avoid the temptation to run off and grab every journal which has an article somehow related to your topic. Read the entries and interpret them carefully. Often, article titles are specific enough to present a relatively clear sense of the article's particular focus. For example, the following titles are both found under the heading Hand in CINAHL: "Burns of the Hands and Arms" and "The Effectiveness of Hand Washing Techniques," the first is clearly related to burns and their treatment, while the latter focuses on medical asepsis. Obviously, one or the other of these articles might be useful in a properly focused research paper, but probably not both. Consult only the useful one and spare yourself a waste of time.

Additionally, the indices are helpful when you've no idea what topic to select. Browse CINAHL, for example, to see if a particular article title or set of articles grabs you. Sometimes skimming an article on an unfamiliar issue will provide direction when you're unsure of where to go.

Avoid consulting the Reader's Guide to Periodical Literature when you are preparing a paper related to your professional studies. The Reader's Guide is a useful tool in other contexts but catalogues primarily popular periodicals aimed at a general readership. Articles listed in the Guide will not, as a rule, be sufficiently developed or documented to be technically accurate, even if they are basically correct in presenting facts. Avoid popular periodicals in preparing a professional technical paper; informative and entertaining all, they are inappropriate sources. The only exception—and a rare one—might be to use articles aimed at popular audiences as supplementary sources or to provide examples. Do so only when you feel you must; otherwise, resist the impulse.

Medline. Another reference tool for locating periodical references is the Medline, a computerized system for literature search. Since Medline is cross-referenced, you can use it to search references on as specific a topic as you need. For example, if you want articles on juvenile diabetes, insulin dependency, you simply tell the computer. When using an index, you must look up diabetes, insulin, and perhaps adolescence, and wade through a list of articles. The major drawback of Medline use is that you must be very specific and match the computer's topics or you get back irrelevant data.

Card catalog. Another tool you'll use to locate potential sources is, of course, the card catalogue. If you're not familiar with its location or use, your librarian will be glad to help with either or both. Use the catalog both to locate and to screen potential textbook sources. Each item your library owns appears under title, author, and topic headings in the card catalog. Typically, the card includes not only basic data such as title, author, and call number, but also sometimes includes a list of alternate topic headings. Use this information to help determine if a given reference might be useful. Ignore potential sources which do not clearly address your topic. Here's a sample:

726.904 Health Care Workers—
G123 Legal Risks

Gregory, John and Diana K. Irvine
Health Care Law: RX for Disaster.
Monterey, California: Brooks Cole Co. 198-
152 p.; 22 cm.

1. Health Care Workers—Legal Risks.
2. Legal Aspects of Health Care.
3. Malpractice and Health Care Workers.
4. Law Suits in Health Care—Case Studies.
5. Title.

In this instance, if you are seeking case studies or information regarding malpractice suits, you'd look more closely at this choice.

Once you've determined that a specific text is probably useful, you're ready to check it out first hand. Don't just sail off, grab it, check it out of the library, and go home, though. Slow down. Follow this procedure.

1. List all the titles and call numbers of texts you think might be useful.
2. Use the locator chart—or ask a librarian—to find the location of the texts by call number.
3. Plan your route through the library based on the locations. This plan isn't necessary, perhaps, in a small library, but in multistory buildings a route plan will save you a good deal of time and sweat. Start at the top and come down, or start at the bottom and go up, but don't jump from floor to floor and back again.
4. Screen each text before you decide to sign it out. Do this to be sure each book contains material you need:
   a. Locate key items in the index, or
   b. Skim the table of contents, if the text has no index.
   c. Check pages listed in the contents or index and skim them.
   d. Put the text back on the shelf unless you're sure it fits your requirements.
   e. Sign out only those texts you are sure you can use.

Don't worry too much if textbook sources are hard to find. Texts are already dated somewhat the day they reach print, and in the allied health professions timeliness is essential. Given the frequency of periodical publication—monthly is most common—journals are likely to be the most timely sources.

Research pitfalls to avoid. Restrict yourself, for the most part, to professional journals, those periodicals aimed directly at individuals studying or practicing in a particular allied health profession. Generally, you should stick to your clinical specialty and level for sources. That is, if you are studying to be an RN, journals aimed at an LPN audience are not usually appropriate choices. The converse is also true. Use caution, too, in using foreign journals. While their approach may offer a new perspective, they tend to be written for an audience whose practice may differ from that in your country. If in doubt about the professional character of a particular journal, check with your instructor or with a librarian. Don't overlook, while you're digging, potential sources from parallel or related professions—anthropology, psychology, sociology, education, for example. Often, professional journals aimed at these audiences offer valuable insight. If you are unsure of the suitability of a given journal, see if it's indexed in any of the three indices: CINAHL, HLI, or IM.

By the way, another pitfall of which to beware, and one into which the unthinking sometimes fall, is the temptation to grab up a year's worth of a particular journal and look through each issue seeking a particular type of article. Don't! You'll be wasting time and energy. Use the topic headings of the index most likely to yield results.

In dealing with most topics, restrict your selection to materials which are no more than five years old. Medical facts change constantly, so using the newest material available is the safest way to ensure accuracy. Older materials are useful for getting background or for tracing developments, but could be misleading as to current practice. An exception would be those texts which are considered standard or definitive in your field of study. These texts often form the basis of more recent materials and are thus reliable.

Primary sources. While you are considering sources, don't overlook primary ones. So far we've discussed only print sources, books, and periodicals. These are secondary sources; others have done the initial work and reported their findings or discussed their views. You are using their comments second hand. Films, microfilm and microfiche, other media such as pamphlets and newspaper, tapes and records, even lecture notes, are all secondary sources.

Primary sources are those with which you work directly. Interviews with clients are a form of primary research, as would be a survey of fellow students. Observations of interactions among clients, observations of results of tests or experiments, testimony by experts or persons who have experienced a particular phenomenon—all are forms of primary research. Your topic might benefit from the use of primary sources. A CVA patient might comment on the effectiveness of certain therapy modes, or other students may have experience with the management of CVA patients. A client might become a case study. While the experiences of such individuals hardly constitute valid scientific proof of a given position, they may reinforce and add interest to that position. Formal laboratory and clinical observation are also primary research, but such studies are beyond the scope of this discussion, as we've said.

Consider using both secondary and primary sources. Select and use only those which you feel are likely to yield useful information. Avoid dabbling with materials which are only peripheral to your topic to save time and energy.

APPLICATION:
Select a potential topic. List 3 potential articles to use as research sources.

Gather Background

Having consulted a dictionary, you've begun to gather background on your topic. This general information should help you to focus your topic selection more closely and clearly. As you define your topic, you learn about its various aspects and can begin to choose your direction.

At this point in the process, encyclopediae may be useful, especially if you have little knowledge of your topic. Use medical encyclopediae, especially, to get a broad idea of the basic concepts or issues surrounding your topic. This information will provide you with a helpful frame of reference as you continue with your research.

Checking the indices to professional periodicals also helps topic focusing. You may find, for example, that nothing has been written lately on the topic you have considered your first choice. Or you may discover that, while many articles exist, your library subscribes to none of the periodicals containing them or that other students have beaten you to them. In such cases you can retool either by shifting your focus or by moving to your next choice of topic.

Your initial research may even tell you that your first choice is irrelevant, boring, or shallow. Again, move on. Avoid spinning wheels wasting time over a topic which resists your efforts. If materials are inaccessible, shift your focus. You may change your tentative topic several times in the course of developing your paper. Such changes are normal, if sometimes a bit frustrating.

Narrow the Focus

Again, the source selection process should help you to narrow the topic you are working. Early on, you should focus on a particular topic and pursue that topic.

Too broad a topic will be impossible to manage. "Stress," for example, is much too broad, a topic perhaps better suited for book-length treatment than a research paper of any but mammoth proportions. "Managing Stress Through Diet" is far more manageable though still somewhat general. "Effects of Salt Consumption on Hypertension" is quite narrow. Focus the topic narrowly enough that you can find useful data and organize them into a readable, comprehensible statement, but don't focus so narrowly that your topic is

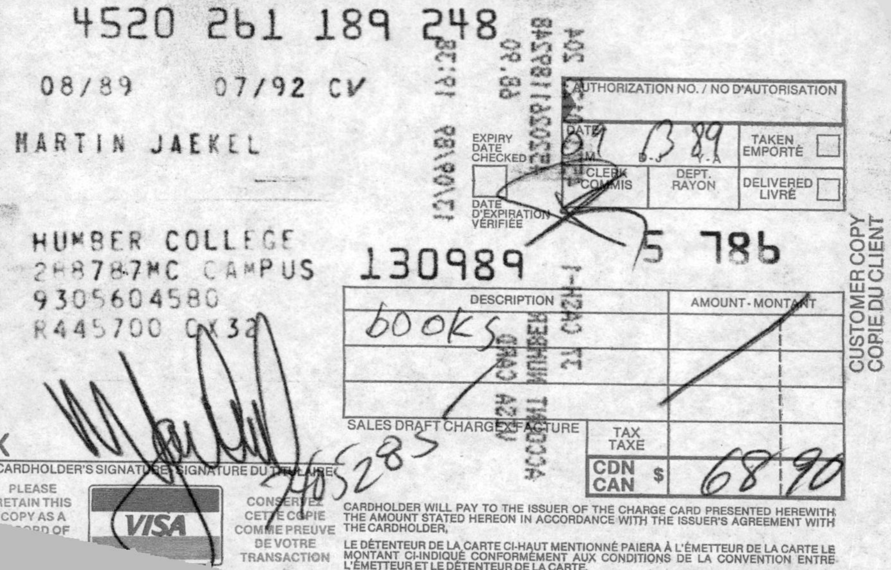

4520 261 189 248

08/89 07/92 CV

MARTIN JAEKEL

HUMBER COLLEGE
2H8787MC CAMPUS
9305604580
R445700 CX32

130989 5 786

13/09/89 19:38
68.90
4520261189248
204

37 CASH-1
ACCOUNT NUMBER
VISA CARD

AUTHORIZATION NO. / NO D'AUTORISATION

DATE 09 13 89
M D-J Y-A

TAKEN EMPORTÉ

CLERK COMMIS

DEPT. RAYON

DELIVERED LIVRÉ

EXPIRY DATE CHECKED

DATE D'EXPIRATION VÉRIFIÉE

DESCRIPTION	AMOUNT - MONTANT
books	

SALES DRAFT CHARGEX FACTURE

TAX TAXE	
CDN CAN $	68 90

X

CARDHOLDER'S SIGNATURE SIGNATURE DU TITULAIRE

405285

PLEASE RETAIN THIS COPY AS A RECORD OF

VISA

CONSERVEZ CETTE COPIE COMME PREUVE DE VOTRE TRANSACTION

CARDHOLDER WILL PAY TO THE ISSUER OF THE CHARGE CARD PRESENTED HEREWITH THE AMOUNT STATED HEREON IN ACCORDANCE WITH THE ISSUER'S AGREEMENT WITH THE CARDHOLDER.

LE DÉTENTEUR DE LA CARTE CI-HAUT MENTIONNÉ PAIERA À L'ÉMETTEUR DE LA CARTE LE MONTANT CI-INDIQUÉ CONFORMÉMENT AUX CONDITIONS DE LA CONVENTION ENTRE L'ÉMETTEUR ET LE DÉTENTEUR DE LA CARTE.

CUSTOMER COPY
COPIE DU CLIENT

too specialized, advanced, or esoteric to be useful.

Below are topics classified as general or focused. Those which are general are too broad to be manageable.

General	Focused
CVA	Physical Therapy in CVA
Stomach Ulcer	Laser Surgery in Treating Peptic Ulcer
Cervical Cancer	Detecting Cervical Cancer Through the Pap Smear
Alzheimer's Disease	Nursing Interventions in Alzheimer's Disease

Consider the assigned length of your paper in focusing your topic. Clearly, the more limited your space the more narrow the limits of your focus. Consider also the effectiveness with which you can address your topic. Treat the topic generally and generally your treatment is superficial.

APPLICATION:
Restate your topic in very specific, narrowly focused terms.

Skim the Sources

Skimming helps in sorting potential sources and in focusing your topic. Moreover, skimming not only prepares you to take notes efficiently and effectively, but also saves you time.

Instead of reading your potential sources word for word and taking copious, diffuse notes, skim first and eliminate any materials which don't offer useful ideas or information. If you weed out such items before taking notes, you save time.

Use skimming also to locate important points within your sources and thus avoid making endless notes on everything you read. As you skim, consider the direction in which your sources are taking your topic and adjust your focus if needed. Skim both periodical and textbook sources.

Follow these guidelines:

1. Read the title of the article or chapter: focus on the major issues to be presented.

2. Read the introduction to identify the major points to be discussed. Usually the introduction presents key ideas in the order of their presentation and prepares you to grasp them more readily.
3. Read the conclusion. In many articles and chapters, the conclusion summarizes or recapitulates major points, sometimes with additional clarification. Now you should know exactly what to look for as you proceed.
4. Skim the body of the article or chapter looking first at subheadings, illustrations, charts, pictures, italicized or bold print, and similar highlighted features. These devices call the reader's attention to the most important issues in the source. As you proceed, they will help you to locate the key points emphasized in the introduction and conclusion.
5. Skim the body again, this time paying particular attention to the discussion of key points you've located. You can safely skip over other contents, having determined their relative unimportance.

During this last phase of the skimming process, you'll make notes to which you'll refer in developing your paper. Again, reading your sources word for word is usually unnecessary in capturing useful notes.

Note Useful Information

Like skimming, making effective notes is not only a helpful skill for the research paper writer, but also a useful study skill for the student who wants to use time effectively. Good notes help you recapture the essence of what you've read, jog your memory so you can recapture the context, and make rereading unnecessary. Good notes are a key element in developing a paper, since they are easier to manage than are the original sources. Additionally, good notes are easier to study than the original sources since the notes already focus on key ideas.

Start by making up a note page or card. Put the required bibliographical data at the top of the page for reference: author, title, place of publication, publisher, and date of publication for texts; author, article title, periodical title, volume, date, and inclusive page numbers of the article for periodicals. You'll need this information later to do your reference notes and bibliography, so doublecheck now for accuracy and completeness. Abbreviate only when standard abbreviations exist. Don't create your own.

Your note page will look like this for a text:

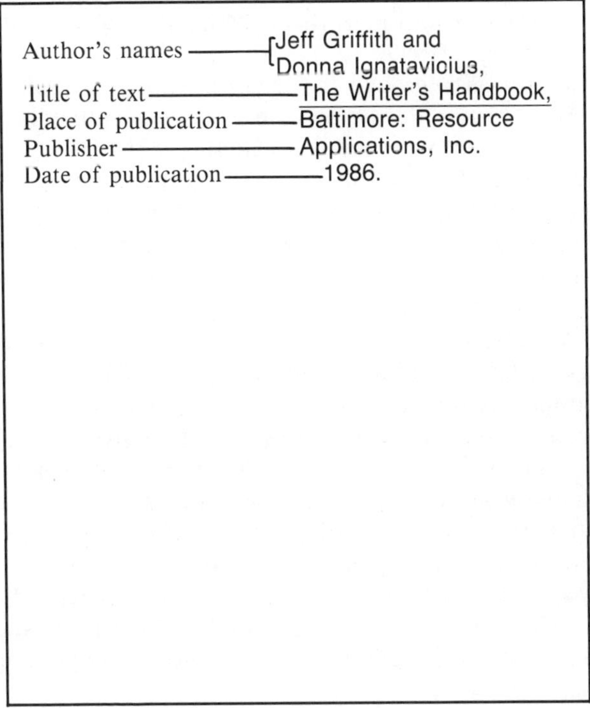

For a periodical, the heading on your note page will look like this:

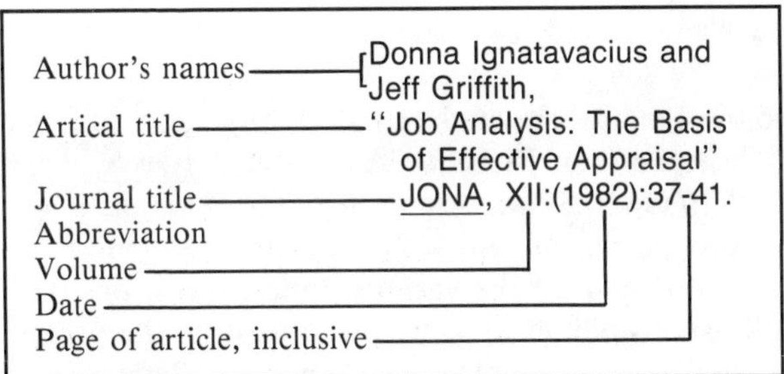

Refrain from making any notes until you've set up the note page: If you forget any of the required bibliographical information, your notes will be useless and you'll end up wasting time going back to the library to relocate your source.

Next write a crisp one or two sentence summary of the source. This will help later as a memory device.

Now, note the page number, for reference, on which you will begin making notes. You'll need this page number later should you need to document a reference to this source.

Finally, proceed through the article as in step five of the skimming procedure, writing down key points you've identified previously. Use direct quotes from your source to capture verbatim statements you feel are critical. Be sure to indicate direct quotes by quotation marks. Otherwise, summarize contents in your own words, quoting key words where necessary. Keep your notes as terse and succinct as possible; remember, all they need do is recapture key ideas. Use direct quotes freely, since they are quite useful in preparing an effective paper, but keep them as brief as possible to capture major ideas. Doublecheck spelling, wording, word order, and punctuation of direct quotes. You must reproduce direct quotes exactly in your paper.

As you move from page to page in your source, be sure to note the page number changes. Draw a line under each page's set of notes, so that you can tell where one page ends and the next begins. Be sure also to label the source of each page of notes you take clearly, so that you don't misplace any information.

As you undoubtedly know, many instructors require the use of 3x5 or 5x8 inch note cards. If you are comfortable with this technique, or if your instructor insists, use it. The note page technique here is an alternative.

The sample note page which follows displays, for part of an article, the process we've just discussed. The article on which these notes are based appears as a sample in Chapter 6.

Sample Note Page

Donna Ignatavicius and Jeff Griffith, "Job Analysis: The Basis of Effective Appraisal," JONA, XII(1982): 37-41. Main idea: Job Analysis is a process which "identifies, specifies, organizes, and displays" the various duties, tasks, or responsibilities actually performed by the person in a given job. This article explains the process step by step.

---

p 37 Job analysis (JA) produces a job description (JD) that "clarifies expectations" and provides a basis for performance appraisal.

3 Benefits

1. JD is the job, not an approximation.
2. process cooperative; leads to open communication.
3. minimizes negative impact of apprasial.

Steps in JA

1. Beginning JA
   Chief nsg exec. should be in charge. Should start with that job.
   Supervisory personnel from all units should participate.
2. Naming the job
   Name job specifically: gives clue to exact nature of job "team leader; orthopedics."
3. Listing DTRs (Duties, Tasks, Responsibilities)
   Each job a set of tasks.
   Task means everything required in performing the job.

---

p 38 Don't hold nurse responsible for task not in job description.

Survey incumbents in jobs: develop lists of actual DTRs.

Observe performance to verify. Don't depend on existing job descriptions.

Specify tasks; don't generalize.

"Sets individual professional development goals cooperatively with unit members" not "assists in development."

Stating DTRs Behaviorally

Use action verb phrases:

"directs the implementation of physician's orders" and qualifiers needed to specify: "by assigning patient care to specific staff members" and "by observing patient care process" includes what nurse does and how nurse does it.

Categorizing DTRs

JDs usually mix tasks illogically: leads to confusion.

---

p 39 To clarify, classify tasks by type.
Examples: direct care, supervisory, maintenence duties to patients, duties to peers.
Derive categories from tasks; don't impose categories.

APPLICATIONS:
Skim a selected article. Prepare a note page and sample notes from at least 2 pages of the article.

Preparing a Precis

A precis, a type of abstract, is a terse summary, the purpose of which is to present the central idea of a specific selected source. You may be assigned precis in your academic activities, or, occasionally, you may wish to prepare a precis professionally. An effective precis presents sufficient detail so that the reader grasps the central idea of the source and gets a reasonably clear idea of the major supporting points presented. In many cases, the precis is value-neutral: that is, the writer presents a straight-forward report of the source's contents without comment. Sometimes, however, the purpose of the precis is to evaluate the usefulness, effectiveness, accuracy, or applicability of a source. In such an instance, the writer presents an evaluation.

Naturally, the process of preparing a precis shares several steps of the research paper process. Unless you are assigned a specific article or topic, screeen and select sources as you would for a larger project. Once you've selected an article which suits your interest, skim and take notes using the techniques outlined here. Once you've completed your notes you're ready to plan. Proceed this way:

1. State the main idea or purpose of the article clearly.
2. Sort your notes; identify the major supporting ideas, illustrations, examples, arguments, or statistics which support and clarify the main idea or purpose.
3. Organize these supporting points in order of importance.

Now you're ready to write. Present in this format:

1. Display the bibliographical information on the top of the page. No title is necessary.
2. State the main idea or purpose of the article immediately. If the article intends to inform a specific audience, say so.
3. Discuss, very briefly, those supporting points you consider most important. Eliminate those which are not absolutely essential.
4. Concentrate on writing crisp sentences and paragraphs. Write a separate paragraph for each major point. Feel free to use direct quotes.
   Reference notes are unnecessary.
5. Restrict your discussion to about one page—8 1/2 x 11—typed.
6. Refrain from commenting on the article unless
   a) your instructor tells you to do so. Ask for specific direction in such a case.
   b) your audience needs the critique.
7. Conclude with a recapitulation of the main idea or purpose.

Sample Precis

Donna Ignatavicius and Jeff Griffith, "Job Analysis: The Basis of Effective Appraisal," Journal of Nursing Administration, XII(1982): 37-41. *Source*

Job analysis is a process which "identifies, specifies, organizes and displays" the various duties, tasks, or responsibilities (DTRs) actually performed by the person in a job. This article explains the process step by step so that, working together, health care supervisors and workers can produce effective job descriptions. *Purpose*

The authors argue that job analysis done cooperatively leads to open communication and, by clarifying expectations about performance, minimizes the negative impact of evaluation.

Job analysis involves the following steps: *Discussion of Major Supporting Points*

Naming the job specifically so that its exact nature is clear. Include the unit where necessary.

Listing DTRs to include all the tasks required in performing the job.

Stating tasks behaviorally, using action verbs to show what the worker does and how to do it.

Categorizing DTRs so that the job description does not mix classes of tasks illogically. Classify tasks by type: direct care, maintenance, or supervisory, for example.

Prioritizing DTRs to clarify which categories of tasks and which individual tasks are most important. This ranking helps both in time management and evaluation.

Evaluating each task for specificity so that each statement is clear and self contained. Statements should say "what," "when," "how," or "why." Avoid phrases such as "as needed" or "other duties as required."

Eliminating and rewriting so that no superfluous DTRs remain and each is perfectly clear.

Setting standards to assist in evaluating DTRs. In some instances, a task analysis is necessary.

Identifying Constraints such as education, union or non-union, training, experience, pay scale. This step places the job in an institutional context.

Summarizing the job to provide a succinct overview.
Preparing the job description to present the job in a readable, accessible format. The authors provide a sample.

Conclusion

Ignatavicius and Griffith emphasize that job analysis is a cooperative project. "The best way to insure clarity is to build consensus," they assert.

Exercises

Exercise 1

Develop a set of notes from any article you select. (You'll need these notes for the exercises in Chapter 9, so save them.)

Exercise 2

Write a precis using the notes you've prepared above.

Selected Readings

Dox, I., Melloni, B.J., & Eisner, G.M. (1979) *Melloni's Illustrated Medical Dictionary,* Baltimore: Williams and Wilkins.

Roth, A. (1982) *The Research Paper: Process, Form, and Function,* Belmont, California: Wadsworth.

Chapter 9
Planning and Writing the Secondary Research Paper

Objectives

After reading chapter and completing the exercises, you should be able to apply the various steps in the process of planning and writing a research paper.

Specifically, in this chapter you learn to:

- Prepare selected research assignments.
- Document research materials.
- Prepare a bibliography.
- Evaluate selected sample papers.

Now that you've selected materials, focused your topic, and developed notes, you're ready to plan and write your paper. Be sure to use this chapter in conjunction with Chapter 8; what's here depends on what's there. If you jump into the process at this stage without benefit of research and notes, you'll short circuit.

Plan and write using this process:

1. Develop a point of view.
2. Plan your discussion.
3. Write.
4. Document.
5. Revise.
6. Type.
7. Proofread.

Remember that these steps are closely interrelated and that, to some extent, you'll be handling them concurrently, so read the whole chapter before you try to master any particular step.

Develop a Point of View

As you skim your sources and note useful information, you begin to focus more and more closely on your topic, gradually developing a clearer sense of direction. This sense will help you form an opinion regarding your topic which will clarify the purpose of your paper. Finish taking notes on all your sources. Then ask yourself, "What opinion do I hold as a result of my research?" Write that opinion down, framing it as clearly as possible. What you've developed is a kind of thesis statement. For example, the point of view of Bea McComas, whose "The Cancer Nutrition Connection" appears as a sample in this chapter, is that individuals can control their own dietary habits and can change their diets to lessen the risk of cancer. Her paper, therfore, explores that issue. Mary Hashagen, whose "Colostomies: Problems and Solutions" also appears as a sample, feels that colostomy patients can lead relatively normal lives if they and their nurses know how to deal with certain fairly predictable problems. Her paper discusses the common problems and presents ways of handling them.

In essence, both writers have arrived at a position based on their research. Their papers are organized around those positions. To the extent that the writer has a clear purpose—to show that controlling one's diet lessens the risk of cancer, to show how colostomy patients can cope—the writer can plan and execute a coherent paper. This point in the process is a good time to clarify your purpose. The opinion you hold, the position you've developed, is the critical focus of your paper. Exploring that point, explaining that opinion or position, is the purpose of your paper. Write the purpose down:

"My paper is to explain how. . . "

"My paper shows why. . ."

Now you're ready to organize your paper.

> APPLICATION:
> Review your notes from several related sources. Decide the major issue or point those sources raise. Frame a point of view statement: "The purpose of my paper is to explain. . ."

Plan your Discussion

First, ask yourself, "Why do I feel the way I do?" or "How have I reached this position?" Then analyze your notes to find the reasons and to arrange them coherently. Sort and organize your notes this way:

1. Review each set of notes.
2. Highlight information which seems important. Use a yellow marker, circle the item, underline it, or mark it with a star, an asterisk, or an arrow. Just be sure you can find it again easily.
3. Decide what order of presentation makes the most sense. Ask, "What's the most important piece of information here? What's the next? The next?" Or, if you are discussing a process or a series of developments, ask, "In what sequence do these things occur?" Number bits of information accordingly; either by order of importance or by occurrence.
4. Combine pieces of information that are closely related. Several sources may present comment on the same key point. In your discussion you can use any or all of them to explain that point. Number all of these pieces the same.
5. Make a list. First, restate your position. Then write concisely, in the order indicated in your notes, each of the bits of information that led you to your point of view. The most efficient way to do this is by stating the idea briefly and listing the sources by author and page number. The list following is part of that from which "The Cancer Nutrition Connection" flows:

Plan: "The Cancer Nutrition Connection"

Position: Individuals can control eating habits and can change diet to lessen cancer risk.

1. Intro.
   —Define Cancer and give stats on prevalence.
   Cancer Facts, 3.
   —Relation of environment and diet.
   Technologies, 6 & 10.
   —"Nutrition status of host"—Tannenbaum.
   LaBuza and Sloan, 439.
2. Causes/Carcinogens.
   —2 steps of cancer development.
   Technologies, 9.
   Shimkin, 1.
   —Additives in diet.
   VanEys, 353.
   "Does everything cause cancer?" 5.
   —Candian Saccharin Study.
   LaBuza and Sloan, 465.
   "Does everything. . . ?" 1,5.
   —Nitrosamines/Sodium Nitrate.
   "Nitrites and Nitrosamines."
   —Methylene Chloride.
   "Decaffeinating Agent," 24.
   —Charcoal.
   "Diet, Nutrition, and Cancer."
   —No safe dose.
   "Does everything. . . ?" 5.

Your plan, an informal outline, says "Here's my position and these are the reasons why," or "I think that. . . because. . . ." Now you're ready to write.

APPLICATION:
Review your notes. Highlight points which support your point of view. Organize those points in order of importance. Develop a plan using the format presented above.

I think that . . . ______________________________

and these are the reasons 1. ______________________

2. ______________________

3. ______________________

Write

Follow your plan closely, being sure to include the points you've listed. Be flexible, though, and don't feel you must adhere absolutely to the plan. As you write, you'll find that certain thoughts will become clearer or will change in importance and you'll want to modify your perspective somewhat. That's fine.

As you begin, consider that your paper should have three readily discernable parts, a beginning, a middle, and an end. The beginning should introduce the purpose of your paper and preview its key points, providing a sense of direction. This type of opening helps the reader comprehend readily, since the reader knows what to look for, what to expect.

The middle of the paper is its body, the major section. Here you must develop your major points using the detail you've derived from your research. Discuss each point fully, but don't belabor. As you shift from point to point, use subheadings, as we've done here, to help guide your reader. Be sure to follow the order you've introduced in the beginning.

The ending should pull your various points together, reinforcing your main idea. An effective ending often restates the major point, then recapitulates, or recaps, the most important supporting points, again in the same order as presented. The effect of the three parts is cumulative.

1. Tell your readers what you're going to tell them.
2. Tell them.
3. Tell them you've told them.

This approach, which some writers disdain, may seem somewhat mechanical and perhaps less than creative. Maybe so. Remember, however, that the purpose of the research paper is neither to amuse, nor to entertain, nor to delight, but rather to inform. The sooner you get to your point, the sooner your reader will get the point. The more guidance you give your reader, the more likely your reader is to understand what you are doing.

The samples included with this chapter illustrate effective beginning, middle, and ending. Refer to them for guidance.

Tips for good beginnings and endings. Your opening should accomplish two things:

1. It should get your reader's attention.
2. It should let your reader know what's coming.

Some effective attention getters include starting with:

— An anecdote, a brief story or episode that leads into your main idea. Case studies are often very useful here.

— A quotation, either from an"expert" or from a patient or client or another health care worker, which captures neatly a key point.

— Some startling statistics or facts which underscore the importance of your topic but which may be little known.

Avoid opening with a question: "How would you feel if. . . ?" Unless you can find one which clearly goes to the heart of your purpose, a question opening will seem a cliché. Avoid, also, opening with a direct purpose statement: "The purpose of this paper is to examine the. . . " The reader's reaction to such a statement is invariably, "Who cares?" The purpose statement is very important, but it should come after the attention getter.

Perhaps the most effective opening contains an overview which lists the key points to be presented after having gotten the reader's attention and having stated the purpose.

Example:

> This paper will explore the question of. . . First we will discuss. . . Next we will consider. . . Finally, we will review. . .

The body of the paper will then develop these points in this order. Such an overview effectively prepares the reader to follow efficiently and comprehend clearly as you proceed with your discussion.

> APPLICATION:
> Using your point of view statement and your plan, write an introduction. Be sure the introduction includes a point by point overview, a clear cut purpose statement, and an attention getter.

Your ending should accomplish three things:

1. It should reinforce your main idea.
2. It should summarize major supporting points.
3. It should create a sense of wholeness; your reader should achieve a sense of whole idea, not a sense of having been left hanging, unsatisfied.

Two techniques for rounding your paper into a satisfying whole are:

— a split anecdote: tell half of the case study as the beginning; develop your body, then come back and complete the case study after you recap. A new, related, anecdote can also work.

— a follow-up quote: some writers even reuse the opening quote to emphasize their point. Choose a quote that creates a sense of finality and echoes your opening.

Whatever you do, don't introduce a totally new idea in your conclusion. If the idea were important, it would have appeared in the body of the essay. An exception, however, is to use the ending to explain how the reader can proceed, that is, what the reader might be able to do about a problem or concern as a result of having become informed.

Handling the body. The beginning and ending frame your paper, but the body is the center of attraction. Here is where the paper succeeds or fails. The body of your paper must:

1. Develop your point fully.
2. Focus only on that point.
3. Proceed smoothly and coherently.
4. Use research data effectively.

Be sure to provide sufficient detail to clarify your main idea. If you've sorted your notes and organized effectively, developing should follow readily. If you feel you have insufficient material, explore additional sources.

The research paper should focus on one major idea, only; all supporting material should be related. Don't stray from the major issue. If, as you write, you begin to create a second major focus, then either revise your purpose statement to include the new focus or decide which of the two main ideas is more important and stick with it. Don't be surprised if your point of view shifts as you develop the paper but be sure when that happens to refocus your purpose statement. Don't scatter your emphasis.

Divide the body of your paragraph into subheadings which reflect the key points given as outlined in your overview. These subheadings remind the reader of the direction you've chosen and enhance the discussion's coherence. Note that the subheadings are the same key words you've listed in your Table of Contents. The sample papers which follow exemplify this approach.

To provide a smooth, coherent flow, use connections—transitions, words, phrases, statements which help the reader to see the relations among supporting ideas. Coherence depends on the reader's ability to relate the various ideas you are presenting. Remember to preview the major supporting points in your introduction; follow that order during the body of the paper to enhance coherence. Additionally, as we've said, use subheads to highlight shifts from point to point. Then consider what kinds of transitional expressions will help: sequence and time terms, first, second, third, then, finally; cause and effect terms, however, nevertheless, therefore; and cumulative terms, additionally, moreover, also. All are useful depending on context.

Use research data to develop and illustrate the issue you are exploring. Balance each supporting point with examples, opinions, facts, statistics, conclusions, or other materials from your sources. Again, if you've sorted and organized effectively, you'll find this easy to do.

Integrating research material with your discussion is critical to the paper's effectiveness. One basic way to integrate is to be sure that the relationships between the research data and your comments are clear. Supply transitions and attribution to do so: "For example, as Griffith and Ignatavicius say, 'Research papers are fun'," contains both. Attribution supplies the reader with the source of the material; the transition connects it to the rest of the paper. We'll consider additional examples in the next section.

To summarize, the research paper contains three parts: the beginning, the middle, and the end. The beginning gets attention and introduces the main idea clearly. Be sure to build in a purpose statement. The middle, or body, develops the major idea fully and coherently, using research material for support. The ending recaps, emphasizing the main idea and creating a sense of wholeness.

Document

To the inexperienced writer, documenting the research paper is probably the most confusing and troublesome aspect of the process. Actually, documentation may be the easiest part, since it requires little analysis or interpretation but is rather a relatively simple mechanical operation.

Formal and arbitrary, documentation involves two aspects:

1. Some form of reference note to identify sources of specific material.
2. A list of sources used to compile the paper.

When to document. Use reference notes to document all material drawn from secondary sources of any kind. Only facts which are common knowledge can be left undocumented. If you are in doubt about whether a particular statement should be documented, then do so.

References notes of three types are in widespread use. Footnotes and endnotes involve numbered reference outside the prose text of the paper; in-text notes are parenthetical references inside the text. Each format is acceptable in a variety of situations, but to be safe you should ask your instructor which format to use.

In-text notes in MLA format. The footnote/endnote format is the superceded Modern Language Association (MLA) documentation style. In 1984, the MLA introduced a revised format which uses parenthetical in-text notes. The American Psychological Association (APA) also uses parenthetical references, but in a slightly different form. Bibliography (reference list) formats vary between the two association as well.

The MLA and APA publish handbooks which fully explain the detailed technical aspects of their documentation styles. The MLA and APA handbooks are musts for any student who engages in serious secondary research writing. The readings at the end of this chapter list the most recent editions available as well as sources of guidance on the new MLA format. The sample papers at the end of this chapter use the new MLA style, which the following discussion explains.

Document all material derived from or based on secondary sources. You may present secondary material in direct quotes, either complete or partial, in indirect quotes, as paraphrase or summary, or as statistics. See the sample papers for examples. In any case, the material will need reference notes to identify its specific source.

Quotations. Direct and indirect quotes should include attribution statements unless closely integrated into the text. The attribution statement identifies the speaker or source. Here are some examples in MLA format.

Complete direct quotes:

As Williams says, "The dietitian's relationship to the patient is critical" (121).

"The dietitian's relationship to the patient," says Williams, "is critical" (121).

"The dietitian's relationship to the patient is critical," says Williams (121).

Note that in each case, a comma or commas separate the attribution phrase, Williams says or says Williams, from the direct quote. In order to produce interest and variety, you may position the attribution phrase before, in the middle of, or after the quoted material. If you place the phrase in the middle, select a break between phrase and clause or clause and clause. If the quote is two or more sentences, you may split the sentences, but place a period after the attribution, like this:

"The dietitian's relationship to the patient is critical," says Williams. "Unfortunately, though, some doctors overlook diet" (121).

By the way, don't use separate sets of quotation marks to quote passages of more than one sentence. Some students feel they should put quotes around each sentence individually, but this strategy is unnecessary and confusing. Simply enclose the entire statement. Put the reference note at the end of the statement, as above, within parentheses and inside the period unless the quote is more than 5 lines and is separated from the text. An example of that situation follows.

Partial direct quotes:

Williams points out that the relationship between dietitian and the client is "critical"(121).

The client-dietitian relationship is "critical," says Williams (121).

In both examples, the writer has shortened the original quote and simply captured the key word without changing the source's substance. The partial direct quote, because of its brevity, is often preferable to the complete direct quote. Use the complete quote if changing it would mar flow or detract from effect. Otherwise the partial quote will suffice. In any case, be sure to surround directly quoted material with quotation marks.

Indirect quotes:

Williams believes that the client-dietitian relationship is most important (121).

The dietitian-client relationship is most important, says Williams (121).

Note that the indirect quote captures the substance of the source, but in your own words. Use indirect quotes for variety, but use direct quotes where the indirect would mar flow or substance. Note also that the indirect quote is basically a paraphrase which includes an attribution phrase.

The reference note for the above example is the number in parentheses which follows the reference: (121). This in-text note refers the reader to the page number of the specific source of the reference. Numbered footnotes are obsolete. Use the parenthetical method instead.

Parenthetical method. The parenthetical method works this way:

- If the author's or authors' names appear in the attribution, simply give the specific page number of the reference in parentheses.
- If the author or authors do not appear in the attribution, include the name(s) in the parentheses: For example: (Williams 121).

In either case, the name(s) of the author(s) and the page number(s) identify a source which you will have listed in the bibliography of your paper. Your reader simply checks the bibliography to identify the source of the information.

Variations on what to include in the parenthetical note depend on the nature of the source and on what you include in your attribution. The trick is simply to provide sufficient information so that readers can easily identify the source. Here are some of the items of importance.

- If your references include two or more works by the same author, include the specific title in your reference. In the attribution, use the full title; in the parentheses, use a shortened form.
- If your references include two or more authors with the same last name, include the first name in either the attribution or the parentheses.
- If you refer to a work by several authors, name up to three in the attribution or parentheses. For more than three, use

the name of the primary author—the first listed—and the abbreviation et al, "and others," like this: (Williams, et al 121).

- If you refer to a work which lists no author, a journal article with no by-line, or a pamphlet with no author named, for example, treat the article or pamphlet title as you would an author's name. Use the title in either the attribution or reference note, as appropriate. You may shorten the title in parentheses if you wish.
- If you refer to a work of more than one volume, mention the volume in either attribution or parentheses, preferably the latter.
- If you refer to a source which presents material alphabetically, such as an encyclopedia or dictionary, omit the page number; your reader won't need it.
- If you refer to the general argument of a work—the thesis of an article or book—rather than to a particular point, omit the page number. This omission tells your reader that you refer to the entire work.
- If you refer to the Bible, a play, or a poem, provide chapter; act, scene, line; or line references respectively. Your reader can then refer to any edition of the work cited.

Long direct quotes

When a direct quote approaches five lines, introduce it with attribution and a colon, and center it or indent it 10 spaces, whichever is easier for you. Ask your instructor whether to single or double space; some prefer single spacing.

Direct quote five lines or more:

Reference notes are absolutely necessary as Griffith and Ignatavicius insist: ***Attribution***

> Document all material derived from second sources. You present secondary material in direct quotes, either complete or partial, in indirect quotes, as paraphrases or summary, or as statistics. . . . In any case the material will need reference notes to identify specific source. (175)

Direct Quotes, Centered

Note that a centered direct quote needs no quotation marks, since centering makes them superfluous. Note also that ellipsis marks, three dots, indicate the omission of irrelevant material. The fourth dot is a period. In this case, place the reference note outside of the period, since the quote is separated from your text.

Render direct quotes precisely as they appear in the source. Double check for exactness. Use ellipsis sparingly, and only when the eliminated material is superfluous, redundant, or irrelevant. When you must insert a word or phrase to clarify, use brackets like this:

> Griffith and Ignatavicius leave the question of spacing open. "Ask your instructor whether to single or double space [a direct quote of five lines or more]," they say. (178).

Statistics

To present statistics, simply incorporate the data into your sentence and provide a reference note. Quotation marks are usually unnecessary. If you wish to present a chart, graph, table, or illustration, the easiest way to document it is to label it with the source directly underneath, as a caption. Be sure to refer to the chart in your discussion and to explain its relevance.

In-text notes in APA format. The alternative to MLA's simplified format is APA's parenthetical in-text note. In this form, you likewise place the reference note right in the text, but with slightly different information:

> The client-dietitian relationship is "critical," says Williams (1984, p. 121).
>
> To some, the client-dietitian relationship is "critical" (Williams, 1984, p. 121).
>
> Williams (1984) believes that the client-dietitian relationship is important (p. 121).
>
> The client-dietitian relationship is most important. (Williams, 1984, p. 121).

As you can see, the contents and placement of the note may vary:

1. Direct quote, with attribution: (date of publication, page).
2. Direct quote, without attribution: (author, date, page).
3. Indirect quote or paraphrase with attribution: (date, page).

4. Indirect quote or paraphrase, without attribution: (author, date, page).

The date appears after the author's name, as in the third example above, when the author's name is included in the attribution. Place the page reference at the end of the sentence, however.

Selection of the form of reference notes varies according to preference or inclination. Check with your instructor whenever you are unsure what format to use. For more detail regarding formats, see the selected readings at the end of this chapter. The sample papers presented here offer numerous examples of MLA format reference note forms labelled for clarification.

Bibliography. Reference notes direct your reader to the specific sources of certain secondary materials in your paper. To complete the package, you must provide your reader with a list, or bibliography, of all the sources you have consulted while preparing your paper.

References, List of Works Consulted, Selected Readings, and other titles are useful, depending on the type of list you provide. Unless you specify, your reader will assume that the list is a complete one. While the formats for the bibliography vary slightly in MLA and APA styles, the content of each item is basically the same.

For periodicals:

- Author, last name first. Use the name of the primary author, the first one listed, where the article lists more than one. In MLA format, don't reverse first and last names of the cooperating authors. Give authors' full first names and initials in MLA style; in APA, give the initials only.
- Title of article, in quotes for MLA, none for APA.
- Title of the periodical, in italicized print or underlined.
- Volume number, underlined for APA.
- Date of publication, year only, in parentheses. Place after author's name for APA; place after volume number in MLA. If no volume is given, give month and day, 2 Feb. 198-, without parentheses in MLA style. For APA, put the month in the parentheses after the year.
- Inclusive page numbers, not just the pages to which you've referred.

For textbooks:

- Author, as above.
- Title of text, italicized or underlined.
- Place of publication.
- Publisher.
- Copyright date (in parentheses after author's name for APA).

Match your bibliography style with your reference note style, MLA or APA. Don't mix. Punctuation and capitalization conventions vary. Use the sample research papers in this chapter as models for MLA style; use the selected readings after this chapter and Chapter 8 as models for APA style.

Organize the bibliography alphabetically by the last names of the primary authors. Where an author's name is unavailable, use the first substantive word in the title to alphabetize. Indent the second and subsequent lines of each entry five spaces, but don't number entries. Doublecheck each item for accuracy and completeness; do the same for your reference notes.

Document as you develop your paper. Simply provide the in-text notes as you write. In no case should you wait until you've completed your discussion and then go back and try to document. You'll waste time that way. The most efficient way to generate your bibliography is to arrange your notes alphabetically and proceed item by item. If you've prepared your note pages or cards properly, all the information you'll need to document is ready and waiting for you.

Revise

The first draft of your research paper is hardly likely to be the last. Plan to complete the initial version far enough in advance so that you'll have time to let it set a few days. Then go back and reread it. As you reread consider these issues:

1. Is the purpose clear?
2. Does the beginning get attention and create focus?
3. Are all references properly documented? All quotes accurate? Integrated?
4. Are all reference notes accurate and complete?
5. Is the body coherently organized?
6. Have I provided sufficient development? Are all the points on my list adequately presented?
7. Does my ending recap? Does it satisfy?

Concentrate now on the effectiveness of your paper. If any of these points reveal a weakness, strengthen that part of the paper. A useful technique is to enlist the aid of a fellow writer. Have your colleague read your draft and point out sections which present problems. Revise accordingly.

In addition, as you reread your paper, check to be sure that all your sentences are complete thoughts and that all spelling is accurate. If any sentences strike you as awkward or unclear, revise them. Finish your revisions before you type the final paper, if you can. Avoid wasting time retyping.

Type

Type your paper if at all possible—some instructors will accept a neatly handwritten paper if you ask, but few will do so enthusiastically. A neatly typed paper is attractive and produces a positive psychological impact.

Your instructor will probably dictate the specific format you are to use, but if not, here's one that's useful: use standard 8-1/2x11 paper, one side only.

> **Title page:** Center the title; put your name underneath; put your class, instructor's name, and date in the lower right hand corner.
>
> **Table of Contents page:** The contents list replaces a formal outline, but gives the reader the same benefit, a quick overview. Center Contents, set a one-inch margin, and list the major sub divisions of the paper. After each, type a line of dots and, on the right, display the page number on which discussion of that concept begins. Leave a one-inch margin on the right as well. Prepare this page after typing the rest of the paper.
>
> **Body of the paper:** Begin page one about two inches from the top; leave one-inch margins all around. Don't number page one. Double space. Begin numbering pages with page two; place the numeral in the center of the top of the page, about 1/2 inch from the top. Again, leave one-inch margins all around, including the top.
>
> **Bibliography page:** Title this page, then triple space to your first entry. Double space each entry; be sure to indent second and subsequent lines. If your instructor says to single space entries, double space between entries. Don't number this page. If your bibliography runs to second or third pages, you needn't title them.

Ask your instructor for guidance on format, but if none is forthcoming, decide on your own. The major goal of presentation should be a consistent, clear, readable product. Once you choose a design, stick to it.

If you turn in a handwritten paper, follow the guidelines above, double space everything, and leave one-inch margins. In either case, avoid the temptation to use wider margins and spacing to make your paper look longer than it really is.

Proofread

Regardless of who types your paper, you are responsible for its contents. Before you turn it in, check for spacing, typographical errors, omissions of content, and other errors. Make corrections neatly, using the symbols discussed in Chapter 1 where applicable. Neat corrections do not mar a paper's quality. Uncorrected errors do.

Research Paper Guidelines

1. Break your project into small pieces and proceed step by step.
2. Screen potential sources. Don't waste time trying to read everything.
3. Zero in on a specific, narrow, topic. The broader your scope, the tougher your job.
4. Skim your sources before you take notes. Eliminate irrelevant sources and irrelevant material within sources.
5. Note materials systematically. Capture all the necessary documentation data, including page numbers, in your notes.
6. Double check direct quotes carefully. Check documentation data as well.
7. Clarify your point of view. Prepare a purpose statement.
8. Plan before you write. Prepare a list of key points and support.
9. Write from your plan, but be flexible.
10. Present an opening which captures interest, a body which develops your main idea fully, and an ending which satisfies.
11. Document thoroughly; double check all quotes and reference notes.
12. Review your first draft after letting it settle. Revise anything that's unclear.
13. Present the paper in a neat, consistent format, preferably typed.
14. Proofread! Typos and careless omissions can kill.

Exercises

Exercise 1

Refer to the sample papers which follow. Select three items from either bibliography; rewrite them in APA format.

Exercise 2

Prepare a sample bibliography using at least four sources you select. Use either format.

Exercise 3

Write a sentence which:

- — includes a complete direct quote.
- — includes a partial direct quote.
- — includes an indirect quote.

Use your notes from Exercise 1 in Chapter 8.

Exercise 4

Document each of the above sentences using both MLA and APA format.

Exercise 5

Select one of the sample papers; evaluate the beginning and ending in terms of the guidelines given in this chapter.

Exercise 6

Select one of the sample papers; evaluate the body in terms of the guidelines given in this chapter.

Selected Readings

Gebaldi, J., and Achert, W.S. (1977) The MLA Style Sheet. New York: The Modern Language Association.

Publication Manual of the American Psychological Association. (1974) 2nd ed. Washington, D.C.: American Psychological Association.

Winkler, Anthony C. and McCuen, J.R. (1985) Writing the Research Paper: A Handbook. 2nd ed. New York: Harcourt, Brace, Jovanovich. Contains updated explanations of MLA and APA formats.

The Cancer Nutrition Connection

Bea McComas

Dt. 102
Professor Gregory
4-8-8-

The Cancer Nutrition Connection

Contents

(REMEMBER: TYPE YOUR PAPER ON STANDARD PAPER, ONE SIDE ONLY.)

McComas
Dt. 102

Introduction

Startling Statistics Used As Attention Getter

Cancer, which can be briefly described as uncontrolled growth and spread of abnormal cells, is the most feared of all human diseases. This year in the U.S. about 430,000 people will die of cancer—1,180 per day, one every 73 seconds. In 1981 an estimated 421,000 died of cancer, 413,000 in 1980, 405,000 in 1979. Cancer is the number one cause of death by disease of children ages three to fourteen (Cancer Facts 3). This steady death rate increase of approximately 7,000 per year has brought about an increased interest in the factors associated with cancer causation and prevention.

Reference To Pamphlet—No Author Given

Studies over the last two decades indicate that 60-90% of all human cancers are associated with the environment and are therefore preventable. Environment encompasses anything that interacts with humans, including substances eaten, drunk, smoked; natural and medical radiation; workplace exposures; drugs; aspects of sexual behavior; and substances present in the air, water, and soil (Technologies 6). The specific reactions between diet and cancer are not fully understood, but diet is considered to be associated with a large percentage of cancers (Technologies 10). Although we do not have control over all the environmental factors associated with cancer causation, we do have direct control over dietary habits and food choices.

- 2 -

McComas
Dt. 102

This paper will deal with the nutritional aspects of cancer causation and prevention. Studies include the effects of carcinogenic substances added to foods, epidemiological studies (studies of population dietary habits), and the specific nutrients—which ones are cancer promoters and which ones are cancer inhibitors. The conclusion will offer dietary guidelines for cancer prevention.

Overview

The link between diet and cancer is not new. In fact, some studies date back as far as the turn of the century. According to Tannenbaum, "These investigations appeared to be based on the concept that since tumors develop from living cells and grow by assimilating nutrients from the host, the nutritional status of the host might be expected to modify the development and growth of neoplasm" (LaBuza and Sloan 439). In other words, the individual has control over dietary habits and their modification as a goal towards cancer prevention.

Reference To Work By Two Authors

<u>The Causes: Carcinogens</u>

Cancer causation involves at least two steps, an early initiation step and a later promotion effect. A single agent may cause both events, or two or more agents working together in a proper sequence may be necessary. The initiation step seems to involve a genetic change in a cell, but the change does not result in a tumor unless a promotion event follows it. The latent period of most cancers—the time between exposure

- 3 - McComas
Dt. 102

to an initiator and appearance of the disease—is often twenty years or more. But this time can be much shorter (Technologies 9). Carcinogenic activity is based on the relationship between the exposure and eventual appearance of a tumor (Shimkin 1).

Reference To Work By One Author

Diet is the major vehicle for toxicants, some of which are carcinogenic (VanEys 353). Three carcinogenic additives which have been proven to cause cancer in laboratory animals are saccharin, sodium nitrite, and the decaffeinating agent in coffee, methylene chloride. Researchers generally agree that a substance which causes cancer in animals represents a risk in humans as well ("Does Everything?").

Reference To Article, No Author Given

An extensive study on saccharin conducted in Canada found that saccharin causes cancer in laboratory rats. Saccharin is now banned in Canada, but is still in use in the U.S. The doses of saccharin which produced bladder cancer in rats in some of the Canadian tests are equivalent to 1,000 diet sodas per day. LaBuza and Sloan report other studies which used doses equivalent to only two diet sodas per day, but which caused cancer of the lymph system and breast tumors in other animal experiments (465). The Food and Drug Administration (F.D.A.) concluded that the consumption of only one diet soda per day by every American could cause an additional 1,200 cases of bladder cancer per year ("Does Everything?" 5). Despite this evidence, opponents of the ban argue that people should have a choice and the government should not interfere.

Widely Published Finding Which Needs No Documentation

Indirect Quote, Authors Identified In Attribution Phrase

- 4 -

McComas
Dt. 102

Nitrosamines, chemicals which cause cancer in laboratory animals, are found in a variety of foods. They are produced when nitrites, which are often added as a preservative, react to amines, which are natural food constituents.

Sodium nitrite is added to 60-90% of all U.S. pork, and is sometimes added to other meats, poultry, fish, cheese, and mushrooms. Of the more than 130 nitrite components tested, 80% caused cancer in laboratory rats. Current law requires that nitrites be banned if found to cause cancer in laboratory animals. The F.D.A. and the United States Department of Agriculture, however, fear an adverse public reaction to an outright ban. Instead they will be phasing out nitrites gradually over the next few years ("Nitrates and Nitrosamines").

Reference to Bulletin, Pages Unnumbered

A newly discovered carcinogen, methylene chloride, a chemical commonly used to decaffeinate coffee, has been found to cause cancer in mice. Methylene chloride has always been a suspect because its chemical structure resembles that of known carcinogens. A water extraction process discovered in Switzerland uses no chemicals to draw caffeine from coffee beans and appears to be the safest bet for decaf drinkers ("Decaffeinating Agent" 24).

Carcinogens can also be produced in meats by charcoal broiling, broiling in the stove, smoking, and sometimes baking at a normal temperature range in the oven ("Diet, Nutrition, and Cancer" 21).

- 5 - McComas
Dt. 102

Note that ingestion of any amount of a cancer causing substance increases the risk of cancer. In other words, there is no safe dose of a carcinogen. As a Health, Education, and Welfare report states, "There is no evidence for a threshold for carcinogenic action, i.e., a dose below which there is no risk of cancer" ("Does Everything?" 5).

Epidemiological Studies:
"The People Factor."

Heredity has often been cited as a reason why people get cancer. Certain data, however, indicate that genetic destiny can be reversed or changed if habits change. Dietary habits are learned behaviors passed down from generation to generation. The reasons that certain families get cancer might not be genes, but rather habits. Air pollution has also been blamed in and of itself for causing cancer. Yet many groups of people enjoy a low cancer rate despite living in heavily polluted areas.

Changes in dietary habits of a population correlate with a changing incidence of cancer among a given population. A classic example is persons of Japanese ancestry who migrated to the United States. VanEys notes that as they changed from their traditional Japanese diet over successive generations to the modern American diet, the incidence of cancer of the breast and colon increased, while cancer of the stomach decreased (353). As the type of diet changed, the type of cancer also changed.

Indirect Quote, Author Given in Attribution

- 6 -

McComas
Dt. 102

Cross cultural comparisons are not uniform among populations worldwide. Variations correlate with dietary habits. Breast and colon cancer, for example, correlate strongly with a higher per capita fat consumption. The theory of fiber content as a preventative shows an inverse relationship ("Diet, Nutrition, and Cancer" 22).

Certain subgroups living in a given population may experience quite different rates of occurrence of cancer. The Mormons, who eat naturally grown produce and naturally raised livestock, and the Seventh Day Adventists, who are strict vegetarians, have much lower cancer rates than others in the same communities who have different dietary habits (VanEys 354).

Indirect Quote, No Attribution

The Nutrients

Based on epidemiological and laboratory studies, scientists have concluded that certain nutrients may be responsible for promoting cancer, while other nutrients act to protect against chemical carcinogens and seem to inhibit cancer development and growth.

High caloric intake and obesity have been linked to tumor genesis. This linkage could be due to an overconsumption of a particular nutrient. The incidence of tumors was lower and lifespan longer, however, for animals on restricted food intake than for animals allowed to eat as much as they desired (VanEys 354).

- 7 - McComas
Dt. 102

Diets high in total fat, whether saturated or polyunsaturated, and diets high in animal source protein seem to increase the risk of cancer. Studies suggest that, when fat intake is low, polyunsaturated fats are more effective than saturated fats in tumor development. The literature on protein is much more limited, yet studies have suggested possible associations between high protein intake and increased cancer risk at several different sites ("Diet, Nutrition, and Cancer" 2).

High intake of dietary salt has been correlated with stomach cancer as with the typical Japanese and Eastern type diets (VanEys 354). On the other hand, as LaBuza and Sloan note, the nutrients that seem to act as cancer inhibitors are the vitamins A, C, E, and trace mineral selinium, and dietary fiber (42).

Pharmacological doses of retinoids—vitamin A and is synthetic analogs, such as beta carotene—fed to experimental animals prevented the development of certain epithelial cancers. Culture studies of carcinogenically induced early cell change in the prostate glands of mice have been reversed by adding retinoids to the culture medium. These studies are extremely important because the majority of cancer in humans is epithelial ("Diet, Nutrition, and Cancer" 23). Carrots, yellow squash, sweet potatoes, and pink grapefruit, among others, are rich in sources of vitamin A.

- 8 -

McComas
Dt. 102

Vitamin E has been shown to inhibit the formation of nitrosamines and other chemical carcinogens ("Diet, Nutrition, and Cancer" 23). Vitamin E functions as an antioxidant protecting vitamins A & C and fatty acids from destruction. It also protects against cell membrane damage, an important factor in cancer formation. Whole grain products, wheat germs, and vegetable oils are rich sources of vitamin E.

The trace mineral selenium also acts as an antioxidant and has been shown to suppress the cancer-causing effects of benzopyrene and other carcinogens. LaBuza and Sloan report that selenite, a form of selenium, lowered the incidence of breast tumors in a strain of mice susceptible to this type of tumor (201). Selenium is found in varying amounts in soil in which vegetables are grown and in water supplies. Individuals should determine if they are receiving adequate amounts of this nutrient.

Dietary fiber, the undigested residue of foods such as fruits, vegetables, and whole grains, has received world wide attention for its role in the prevention of colon cancer. The consumption of some high fiber containing ingredients, such as cellulose and bran, inhibits induction of colon cancer by certain chemical carcinogens ("Diet, Nutrition, and Cancer" 22).

This Reference Documents The Entire Paragraph

Dietary Guidelines

Based on the above studies, the National Academy of Science suggests the following guidelines that may help reduce the overall risk of developing cancer:

- Reduce the consumption of fat, both saturated and unsaturated, to 30 percent of caloric intake;
- Eat fruits, vegetables, and whole grain products everyday, especially foods high in vitamin C and beta-carotene, such as citrus fruits and dark green and yellow vegetables.
- Eat very little salt-cured, salt-packed, or smoked foods such as smoked sausage, smoked fish, bacon, bologna, or hot dogs;
- Drink alcohol in moderation, particularly if a cigarette smoker. ("Diet—Cancer Connection" 3-4)

Summary

Cancer is a very complex disease presenting many variables. Evidence suggests that human cancer results from diet. VanEys contends that, just as cancer and its host are not physically separable, diet and nutrition are not truly separable from an overall lifestyle or from a specific environment (354). We individuals may alter our chances of developing cancer by modifying our food choices nonetheless.

Restatement of Main Idea

No particular food group is harmful in and of itself. Perhaps the problem lies in overconsumption and neglect. For instance, fast food menus consist heavily of fat and protein, but are very neglectful of the fruit,

Recapitulation of Key Points

- 10 - McComas
Dt. 102

vegetable, and grain groups. Yet many Americans subsist on this type of diet.

Besides modifying our own diets, we can have an important input in improving the present food situation. For example, we can:

- Write to our senators, congressmen, and the F.D.A. and let them know how we feel about carcinogenic additives being added to foods.
- Obtain a food additive dictionary and use it while shopping.
- Avoid foods that contain unwholesome ingredients; if consumers don't buy, companies won't make.
- Write to individual companies to complain and offer suggestions when dissatisfied with their products; also compliment them when products are good.
- Read and gather information daily to keep up with new discoveries pertaining to nutrition and health.

To specify a diet that will protect everyone against all forms of cancer is not yet possible. However, cancer has often been described as a man made disease. If man started it, then man can wipe it out. Each of us can help ourselves.

- 11 -

McComas
Dt. 102

Bibliography

American Cancer Society. Cancer Fats and Figures. 1982

Pamphlet, Corporate Author

"Decaffeinating Agent Causes Cancer in Rats." Nutrition Action 9 (1982): 4.

Periodical Reference; No Author Given

"Diet, Nutrition, Cancer." Nutrition Today 17 (1982): 20-5.

"Does Everything Cause Cancer?" Nutrition Action 6 (1979): 3-7.

LeBuza, Theodore P. and Elisabeth A. Sloan. Contemporary Nutrition Consequences. St. Paul: West, 1979.

Textbook Reference; Two Authors

"Nitrates and Nitrosamines." Carcinogenic Information Bulletin 7 (1979).

"Report Details Diet—Cancer Connection." Nutrition Action 9 (1982): 3-4.

Shimkin, Michael B. Science and Cancer. Washington: U.S. Department of Health and Human Sciences, 1980.

Textbook Reference; One Author

Technologies for Determining Cancer Risks from the Environment. Washington: Congress of the United States Office of Technology Assessment, 1981.

Textbook; Corporate Author; Alternate Form (see corporate author reference above)

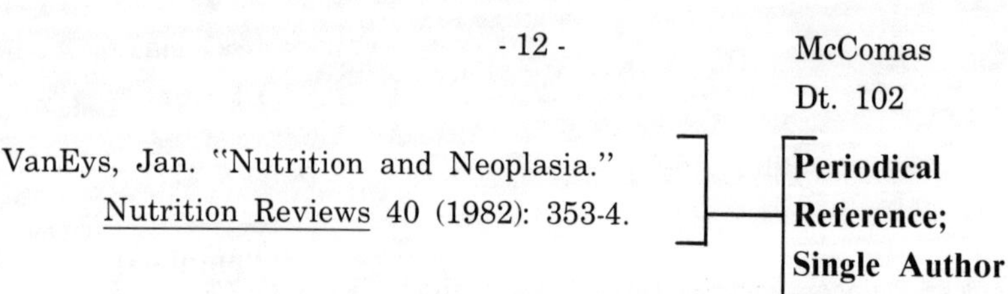
- 12 -
McComas
Dt. 102
VanEys, Jan. "Nutrition and Neoplasia." Nutrition Reviews 40 (1982): 353-4.
Periodical Reference; Single Author

COLOSTOMIES:
PROBLEMS AND SOLUTIONS

Mary Hashagen

Jeff Griffith
N. 202
4-8-8-

Contents

(REMEMBER: One Side Only)

Hashagen
N 202

Colostomies: Problems and Solutions

Anecdote Opening, Based on Case Study

> Joe Stevens has just been told that he has colo-rectal cancer and that he will have to have a colostomy. The shock has left him confused and upset. He realizes that such an operation will change his health habits and his pattern of daily living. (Davidson 14)

Main Idea and Overview

Joe Stevens is a statistic. As a colostomy patient he faces numerous difficulties. This paper will discuss problems that arise with colostomy patients and suggest methods to assist nurses in helping resolve these problems: emotional adjustment, patient teaching, diet control, and self care of skin irritations.

Emotional adjustment

The colostomy patient usually has some difficulty adjusting emotionally. In one case study, Ann Jones tells of her patient's adjustment to the colostomy. She states, "I explained about the colostomy and encouraged her to look at it but she refused." Jones continues, "Over the next two days, Mrs. Miles gained more independence. Although she looked at her colostomy she did not accept it as a part of herself" (54). Luckman and Sorensen explain one of the reasons for this type of behavior:

> Feces are associated in most people's minds with 'dirt' and shame, and

-2- Hashagen
N 202

> bowel movements become a private function quite early in life. Depending upon the individual's attitude toward excretory functions, knowledge about colostomies prior to surgery, and general ability to adjust to stressful situations, the patient's reactions may range from apparently easy acceptance to a total withdrawal from social contacts. (1408)

Quote of 5 Lines Or more

To deal with such emotional problems is difficult, as Davidson points out. "Because the function of the bowels is a very private matter, patients often feel embarrassed about discussing their problems. Therefore," she says, ". . . the nurse [must] establish a good relationship with the patient and his family as soon as possible" (16).

Ellipsis Used To Eliminate Unneeded Part Of Direct Quote; Brackets Used To Insert Word To Enhance Flow

To establish such a relationship, the nurse answers any questions the patient might have, attempts to resolve concerns or worries, explains procedures fully, and encourages the patient to ask questions. Luckman and Sorensen point out that "the nurse's reaction and manner towards the patient and the care the patient requires can affect the person's adjustment" (1408). Dugas adds that the nurse's "calm acceptance of the situation" and "care to protect the patient's feelings of dignity" are essential in attempting to reassure the patient (533). Davidson also adds:

Partial Direct Quote, Integrated Into The Text

> With good medical care, considerate and thoughtful advice from the health

- 3 - Hashagen
N 202

> care staff, loving attention and encouragement from family and friends, a patient should develop enough self confidence to resume normal everyday activity. (18)

Patient Teaching

The patient must learn the proper procedures for self care after the hospital stay. Larson writes:

> Too often we instruct a patient about something, ask if there are any questions, and dash off to our next responsibility. Later on, often at home, the patient discovers he did not understand enough even to be able to ask a sensible question. (iii)

All members of the nursing staff should teach the patient to manage his ostomy with the greatest amount of success possible. Mason states that "visual aids" such as films, charts, slides, and talking models are available in many areas. Visits from persons who have made a successful adjustment to an ostomy are usually of great value to the patient (323). Lectures, exhibits, and literature also aid in adjusting and teaching the patient. Luckman and Sorensen state an important point, "Teaching 'must' be paced to the patient's level of acceptance of the colostomy as well as the ability to perform the tasks of management" (1409). The nursing staff must repeat information several times to ensure that the patient completely understands. To demonstrate competence, the

- 4 - Hashagen
N 202

patient must be able to carry out the procedure properly. Luckman and Sorensen add:

> Many hospitals and some health agencies employ an Enterostomal Therapist who is a registered nurse with postgraduate training in the management of 'ostomies'. This health worker (a) assists patients in finding equipment to meet their needs and (b) usually conducts teaching sessions with patients and with other nurses concerning proper management of ostomies. (1409)

Use Single Quotation Marks To Show A Quote Within A Quote

Diet control

Diet is a possible problem for colostomy patients, because of gas, diarrhea, and hard stools. Larson states, "Adding new foods one at a time will allow the patient to determine if a particular item is a troublemaker and should be avoided" (16). Foods likely to cause gas, says Larson, are onions, cabbage, dried beans, cauliflower, chocolate, and fatty or rich food such as gravies, pastries, and french-fried or deep fried foods (16). Moreover, Luckman and Sorensen write, "Roughage, fresh fruits, and other laxative or bulk forming foods [should] be eaten judiciously or diarrhea may develop" (1411). To remedy this problem Larson notes that "each person has to determine for himself whether a specific food must be avoided. If certain foods have never agreed with the patient, there is no reason to expect that this will change after surgery" (16).

- 5 - Hashagen
N 202

Self Care of Skin Irritations and Strictures

The immediate area of a stoma often gets irritated due to frequent removal of adhesive colostomy bags. Mason suggests the following:

> Substances such as plain tincture of benzoin, calamine lotion, or milk of magnesia may be applied to the skin and allowed to dry before the cement is applied. Tincture of benzoin should not be used if the patient's skin appears to be irritated because of the possibility of further irritation. An antacid, such as magnesium and aluminum hydroxides plus simethicone (maalox) or Karaya powder may be used on the excoriated skin. (425)

To prevent irritation, Larson suggests putting baby powder on the skin around the stoma, covering with a soft paper napkin, cutting an open for the stoma, and then applying the pouch (14). This procedure adds to the patient's comfort, especially in hot and humid weather.

To prevent strictures, the closing of the rectus muscle over an artificial opening, the patient must learn to dilate the stoma with a gloved finger before each irrigation (Luckman and Sorensen 1411).

- 6 - Hashagen
N 202

Summary

Emotion, education, diet, skin irritation, and strictures are but a few of the many problems the colostomy patient faces. Many patients like Joe Stevens and Mrs. Miles can live happy and normal lives, as long as they follow the doctor's orders and practice what they are taught.

Recap

Cycle Ending, Referring to Anecdote Opening

- 7 -

Hashagen
N 202

Bibliography

Davidson, Dorothy. "The Colostomy Patient: Part 1: Nursing Concerns and Considerations." The Journal of Practical Nursing 29 (1979): 14-20.

Dugas, Beverly. Introduction to Patient Care. Philadelphia: W.B. Saunders, 1977.

Jones, Ann. "Only a Temporary Measure?" Nursing Mirror 153 (1981): 52-4.

Larson, Darlene. Living Comfortably With Your Colostomy. Minneapolis: The American Rehabilitation Foundation, 1970.

Luckman, Joan, and Karen Sorensen. Medical Surgical Nursing. Philadelphia: W.B. Saunders, 1980.

Mason, Mildred. Basic Medical-Surgical Nursing. New York: Macmillan, 1978.